This book belongs to

_____

*a woman whose confidence
is in the Lord.*

QUIET CONFIDENCE FOR A WOMAN'S HEART

Elizabeth George

HARVEST HOUSE PUBLISHERS

EUGENE, OREGON

Cover photo © Harry Langdon

Cover by Dugan Design Group, Bloomington, Minnesota

QUIET CONFIDENCE FOR A WOMAN'S HEART
(Formerly published as *Powerful Promises for Every Woman* and
Powerful Promises for Every Woman Growth and Study Guide.)
Copyright © 2000/2003 by Elizabeth George
Published 2009 by Harvest House Publishers
Eugene, Oregon 97402
www.harvesthousepublishers.com

Library of Congress Cataloging-in-Publication Data

George, Elizabeth.
   [Powerful promises for every woman]
   Quiet confidence for a woman's heart / Elizabeth George.
      p. cm.
   Originally published: Powerful promises for every woman. Eugene, Or.: Harvest House, 2003.
   Includes bibliographical references.
   ISBN 978-0-7369-2389-7 (pbk.)
   1. Women—Religious life. 2. Bible O.T. Psalms XXIII—Criticism, interpretation, etc. I. Title.
   BV4527.G4595 2009
   242'.643—dc22

                                                                                    2008045615

Printed in the United States of America

09 10 11 12 13 14 15 / VP-NI / 10 9 8 7 6 5 4 3 2 1

*Thank you to Jim George,
my husband and friend,
for your able assistance, suggestions,
and guidance throughout this project.*

Contents

Questions and Insights
for Deeper Understanding and Discussion

God Is Your Confidence, Hope, and Joy

He will feed His flock like a shepherd.

ISAIAH 40:11

I am the good shepherd. The good shepherd gives His life for the sheep.

JOHN 10:11

Are you in need of strength, guidance, peace, and hope as you make your way through life? I understand. I've been there too. But I have great news! God has powerful promises just for you. We're going to take a close look at 12 of His wonderful, confidence-building promises, so prepare your heart to discover life-changing truths—

- ☙ about the Person and character of God
- ☙ about God's faithfulness to His own
- ☙ about the great promises found in Psalm 23
- ☙ about the moment-by-moment application of

these 12 promises to the issues and trials of your
daily life

Truly, you and I are most blessed to possess the promises of
God to see us through every day and every problem that will ever
come our way.

And to help you get even more out of the truths in Psalm 23 and
this book, a study guide for personal reflection, application, and
digging deeper is included at the end of this book. You can enjoy
this study alone in your quiet time or in a group. These questions
and additional insights will propel you down the path toward a better
understanding of God's complete provision for you.

Psalm 23

How I cherish the simple-yet-all-encompassing truths of the
Twenty-third Psalm. This "Shepherd Psalm" is so life-affirming and
life-changing! I enjoyed sharing these truths with my daughters when
they were growing up. And I know how they love passing them on
to their little ones today. As you and I explore who the Shepherd
is and what that means to us, our lives will be transformed. We'll
become more confident in who (Whose!) we are and what we're
doing in our lives.

～ Building Your Confidence in Him ～

Where does life find you today? What season are
you in?

⤙ *Spring*—Are you in the early beginnings of
life? Are you tasting the joy of fresh starts and
taking your first steps as a Christian?

⤙ *Summer*—Have you progressed along the

way with the Lord to the place of wisdom, of a blossoming knowledge of the One you walk with?

ᴗ *Fall*—Are you in a fast-paced, terrific season of tremendous fruit-bearing, of harvest, of reaping profusely from the benefits that come from a close, sustained walk with God over time?

ᴗ *Winter*—Are you experiencing endings that for the first time seem to have no new beginnings? Are you being pressed to adjust to a new path that leads in directions you didn't anticipate or choose? Are you approaching the next bend in the path with a measure of fear?

As I wrote these words, I was walking through several seasons of life at the same time. In the winter of sorrows and losses, my dear dad died (and so did my husband's mother). My mother was institutionalized and no longer recognized me in any way. Yet it was also the spring of new beginnings. I welcomed my first two grandbabies—one month apart. And I relished a time of great productivity as I enjoyed health and ample time to write and speak to my heart's content.

Just like you, I need God's promises for the seasons I experience. I need them today and for the times I have yet to brave. Isn't it wonderful that we have a God—a loving Shepherd!—that watches over us? His care is unceasing. His love is unending. His guidance is unfailing. His presence is everlasting. We can thank Him too for the promises He gives us in the Shepherd

Psalm that confirm our hope and strength and joy in Him as we grow through and weather the seasons of life. As the psalm's precious fourth verse promises: God is with us every day and all the way.

⤳⤳⤳

David, the Psalmist

When I pick up a book, I always check the backcover or flyleaf for information about the author. I want to know what qualifies the author to write on the subject before I dig in. Have you wondered about the life and the seasons of the writer of Psalm 23? I have. So who is the author and what qualifies him to write it?

King David, the inspired writer of Psalm 23, knew the refreshing seasons of youth, and he knew the maturity of years. But he also experienced...

- ⤳ *a season of rejection...*when expelled from his home and throne

- ⤳ *a season of fear...*when fleeing from the murderous King Saul

- ⤳ *a season of discouragement...*as an anointed king, yet a homeless fugitive

- ⤳ *a season of disappointment...*when God didn't allow him to build the temple

- ⤳ *a season of heartbreak...*as he suffered the death of an infant son and witnessed strife and death among his children

Yes, David's life reveals many strengths and accomplishments. The finest thing said about David is that he was *a man of great faith*. David was not only an ancestor of Jesus Christ, but he was also described by God as "a man after My own heart, who will do all My will" (Acts 13:22). A thousand years later, David, the man of great faith, was honored with a listing in God's "Hall of Faith" (Hebrews 11).

Yet, just as a coin has two sides, so does David. You see, he was also *a man of great failure,* a man who fell into sin. David committed adultery with Bathsheba and arranged for the murder of her husband (2 Samuel 11). Still another of David's failures was his choice to directly disobey God and take a census of the people (2 Samuel 24).

❧ *Building Your Confidence in Him* ❧

As you and I walk through Psalm 23, we'll be stopping many times to consider the life lessons we're discovering. So far our brief look at David, a man of faith and failure, offers these specific instructions.

Lesson #1—David admitted his failures

To the prophet Nathan, David confessed, "I have sinned against the LORD." Then we're told the good news that the Lord marvelously "put away" David's sin (2 Samuel 12:13). The Bible makes it wonderfully clear that the person "who covers his sins will not prosper, but whoever confesses and forsakes them will have mercy" (Proverbs 28:13).

Are there any unconfessed sins in your life, dear friend? As the famous British preacher Charles H. Spurgeon once counseled, "Let us go to Calvary to learn how we may be forgiven." That's good advice for us as New Testament believers. At Calvary, at the cross,

Jesus Christ truly paid it all—the total penalty and price for our sins. Our responsibility now is to confess our sins. His promise is to forgive. And, beloved, there is no sin too great for Him to forgive!

One more thought: After David admitted his failure, the joy of his salvation was restored. His sins were washed whiter than snow (Psalm 51). These same joys await you and me each and every time we acknowledge our transgressions.

Lesson #2—David suffered sin's consequences

Although David was forgiven by God, he paid a price for his disobedience. Consider this classic illustration: You can drive nails into a board, and then you can remove the nails, but the nail holes—the scars—remain. David's life was scarred by his sinful failures. One of his sons died in infancy, one of his sons betrayed him, and his family was divided. David definitely suffered.

These heartfelt words by two authors I admire inspire me. They take into consideration the reality of sin's consequences upon our lives. Anne Ortlund writes, "In my heart I do have a fear...I long to grow more godly with each passing day. Call it 'the fear of the Lord,' being in awe of Him and scared to death of any sin that would mar my life."[1] Carole Mayhall shares, "Daily I live with [one] fear—a healthy fear if there is such a thing. [It is] that I will miss something God has for me in this life. And it is mind-expanding to contemplate all that He wants me to have. I don't want to be robbed of even one of God's riches by not taking time to let Him invade my life. By not listening to what He is telling me."[2]

Why not join these two women in their "healthy fear" of the life-marring sins that can cause you to miss God's best, that can hinder your desire to walk with Him in all His ways? And if you're already bearing the scars of sinful ways, thank the Lord for His amazing gift of forgiveness and His marvelous grace that let's you live for Him from this point forward.

Lesson #3—David went on

After the death of his child with Bathsheba, "David arose from the ground, washed and anointed himself, and changed his clothes; and he went into the house of the LORD and worshiped...and he ate" (2 Samuel 12:20). A forgiven sinner, the grateful David went on to write many poignant psalms, including songs that express his passionate outpouring of confession, a contrite spirit, and the sparkling brilliance of joy.

David harbored no bitterness toward God. He accepted the responsibility for his wrongdoings. He wrote, "I acknowledge my transgressions, and my sin is ever before me. Against You [God], You only, have I sinned, and done this evil in Your sight—that You may be found just when You speak, and blameless when You judge" (Psalm 51:3-4). David owned his sin and considered the Lord to be "gracious...and righteous; yes...[and] merciful" (Psalm 116:5).

Follow David's example of going on after a season of sin or tragedy. Do you need to...

- ✍ get up—rise up from the ground?
- ✍ wash up—wash yourself?
- ✍ dress up—change clothes?

⋙ look up—enter into the presence of the Lord?

⋙ pray up—spend time in prayer and worship?

⋙ eat up—take in nourishment?

⋙ go on—move forward?

What marvelous instruction and resolve you can draw from dear David! He shows you a pattern for spiritual growth: Your role is to rise up and go on. God's role is to sustain you along the way...and He promises to do just that!

⋙

These truths are a powerful prompt to *lift up* your praise to God, *rise up,* and *go on* your journey with the Lord. Your confidence in Him will grow as you explore and claim the promises God offers to you in this brief (only 117 words!) psalm of encouragement and refreshment.

Thank God, your Shepherd,
that His care is unceasing, His love is unending,
His guidance is unfailing, and
His presence is everlasting.

1

God Cares for You

The LORD is my shepherd.

PSALM 23:1

*I am the good shepherd; and I know My sheep,
and am known by My own.*

JOHN 10:14

No words ever written carry the comforting weight these five do: "The LORD is my shepherd." We're soothed and assured by the knowledge and confirmation that God is our personal Shepherd who will care for us and be with us through every joy and challenge of life. I know because I've seen and experienced it myself.

When I led a study on this remarkable psalm for the women's Bible study at our church, the hearts of those who listened were touched again and again by the thought of the Lord as their own caring shepherd. What kind of women were in our group? Women...

- denied the joys of motherhood or whose nests overflowed
- with children who spurned much-needed advice

- ⚒ raising children alone or caring for elderly parents

- ⚒ facing illnesses and life-threatening diseases

- ⚒ coping with physical limitations

- ⚒ struggling with finances or had husbands not working

- ⚒ in unhappy marriages or facing divorce

- ⚒ juggling careers and home life

From every walk and season of life, these were women who loved and needed the loving care of their Shepherd.

Have you ever wondered how the thought of God as a shepherd originated? In Hebrew, the five English words, "*the Lord is my shepherd*," are translated from two words: *Jehovah-Rohi*.

Jehovah-Rohi Feeds, Leads, and Warns

One major meaning of the word *shepherd* is "to feed." Feeding is found throughout Scripture.

- ⚒ The Bible narrative of Joseph opens with him "*feeding* the flock with his brothers" (Genesis 37:2).

- ⚒ Later, in Egypt, when Pharaoh asked Joseph's brothers about their occupation, they answered, "Your servants are shepherds...[and we] have no *pasture* for [our] flocks" (Genesis 47:3-4).

- ⚒ David "returned from Saul to *feed* his father's sheep" (1 Samuel 17:15).

- ⚒ And in the Shepherd Psalm, we read David's inspired words, "The LORD [Jehovah] is my *shepherd*."

✑ *Building Your Confidence in Him* ✑

As one of *Jehovah-Rohi's* sheep, God promises to feed you. As creatures who need physical and spiritual food, we enjoy both from the hands of our loving Shepherd. He cares for us, bringing us to places of green pasture. Through circumstances and events He ensures we're brought to places where we can eat the best and most nourishing foods physically and spiritually.

I'm not a shepherd, but I did work at The Brandeis Institute, located in the rolling hills of Simi Valley, California. The lush hills were part of many sheepherders' routes. At the Institute, the bell at the entrance gate would frequently ring in the spring as yet another caring and loving shepherd asked permission to graze his sheep on the healthy and lush grass.

This kind of care is the role of a good shepherd—and a role completely fulfilled for us by our Good Shepherd.

And here's another tender fact about a good shepherd. When there are no pastures, he gathers the food needed for his flock by using his crook to pull down leaves and berries from trees. Then he feeds his sheep directly from his own hands.

So why do we worry? Why do we worry about food and clothing? About finances and money? About security and the needs of life? We have *Jehovah-Rohi!* We have the Lord as our caring Shepherd. When fears regarding the cares of this world set in, we need to confidently lean on God's promise to care for us. Then we can declare to God, "Whenever I am afraid, I will trust in You" (Psalm 56:3).

⤳⚊

Another way *shepherd* is used in the Bible is in a figurative sense to signify the leadership role of a prince with his people. To David, the Israelites said: "You were the one who led Israel out and brought them in; and the LORD said to you, 'You shall *shepherd* My people Israel, and be ruler over Israel'" (2 Samuel 5:2).

⤳ *Building Your Confidence in Him* ⤳

What a glorious thought—to know you are led! Indeed, your Shepherd is a gentle, patient, and firm guide. And because of His character, you don't need to know the path, the plan, or the future. You only need to know *Jehovah-Rohi*, the God who promises to care for you and to lead you. You can trust Him!

I know as a wife how important my husband's leadership is and the security that following him brings to my anxious heart. When I'm headed toward the falling-apart stage, Jim simply puts his arms around me and says, "Everything will be all right." He doesn't tell me *how* everything will be all right, *when* everything will be all right, *who* is going to make everything all right, or *what* is going to happen to make everything all right. He just assures me that everything *will be* all right. And I am comforted just because my earthly leader, my husband, tells me so.

And, my friend, the assurance is even stronger with

Jehovah-Rohi. He is our Shepherd, our heavenly leader. He is all-knowing and all-powerful. Therefore we need no details. We need only to follow, knowing everything will be all right.

The Lord *is* leading us—there's no doubt about that. But you and I must ask, "What kind of follower am I?" Or perhaps, "Which of these three kinds of sheep am I?"

Restless and discontent sheep: These sheep jump into other fields or climb into bushes and onto leaning trees. They sometimes fall and break their legs. They're nervous and dissatisfied and cause the shepherd endless trouble.

Are you settled—at home with and abiding in the Shepherd? Are you one who trusts…and rests…in the Lord? Is the Lord all that you need? Are you content to be nothing more than His sheep and delight in what He gives you?

Worldling sheep: These sheep are intent on their own pleasures and selfish interests that have nothing to do with the shepherd. They run from bush to bush, searching for variety and sampling every kind of food. Only now and then do they lift their heads to see where the Shepherd is—to make sure they don't wander too far away.

Worldlings dabble in sin and pleasure. They nibble on what is meaningless and even harmful. They stray farther and farther from the good shepherd. There is the "checking in," but then back into the world they go.

Do you want a closer, more confident walk with

God? Draw nearer to God by heeding these time-honored, oft-proven, surefire practices:

- ⚐ Follow the Shepherd. Determine to obey God's Word (John 10:27).
- ⚐ Talk to the Shepherd. Pray always (Psalm 116:1-2).
- ⚐ Listen to the Shepherd. Saturate your soul with God's Word (John 10:2-5).
- ⚐ "Chew" on the Shepherd's food. Memorize and meditate on His Word (Psalm 1:1-2).

Devoted sheep: Blessed is the sheep who always keeps near the shepherd! Each sheep in a flock has a name, and the devoted followers answer joyfully whenever the shepherd calls. By prolonged and continued fellowship, the sheep who follow nearby enjoy the shepherd's presence and become his familiar companions. To those closest to him, he shares the choicest portions of the food he's gathered.

These happy and content sheep are never in danger. Why? Because they are near the shepherd! They will not get lost, fall into mischief, or suffer harm from wild beasts or thieves. Why? Once again, because of their nearness to the shepherd.

How about you? Are you a sheep who stays near the Shepherd? Do you delight in His company? Are you one who says "I am His and He is mine"? If you are, then you will be shown the path of life. You will know fullness of joy in His presence. And you will experience untold pleasures at His right hand forevermore (Psalm 16:11).

Yet another figurative use of *rohi* is in regard to folly and judgment. The Scriptures teach us:

- ↘ "The mouth of fools *feeds* on foolishness" (Proverbs 15:14).
- ↘ The idolater "*feeds* on ashes" (Isaiah 44:20).
- ↘ God will "*feed*" false shepherds "in judgment" (Ezekiel 34:16).

We are warned not to consume, partake of, or be involved in activities that don't exalt God.

⟿ *Building Your Confidence in Him* ⟿

As you follow close to God and delight in *Him* (rather than in foolishness and ashes), you are safe from God's judgment and the results of such dangerous nibbling. You see, with *Him* there is true substance, real meaning. Let me tell you a story—a true story.

My wonderful daughter Courtney moved with her husband, Paul, to Kauai, Hawaii, immediately after their honeymoon. Known as "the garden isle," Kauai is sparsely populated and quite removed from world traffic. Almost everything is imported, which meant that Courtney, an avid reader, had little choice of books to read (and even less money to buy them as a newlywed living in one of the most expensive regions of the United States).

When Jim and I went to visit Courtney and Paul in their home in Kapaa, I was surprised to discover that she was reading through the many books written by Louis L'Amour. In case you don't know about Louis L'Amour, he's one of the foremost and prolific writers of Western fiction. His books are good, factual, well-written, and clean (all reasons why Courtney had chosen them). Also, as Courtney explained, they were available at the public library.

When I returned to the mainland, I voiced my uncertainty about Courtney's reading matter to a friend in Christ. While there's nothing wrong with Louis L'Amour's tales of the Wild West per se, I was concerned that they had become her mainstay. Louis L'Amour's stories were *not* why Jim and I had sacrificed to put our girls through Christian schools from preschool through grade twelve, followed by five years each at a Christian college.

Louis L'Amour's sagas were *not* why we made sure our girls were actively involved in a strong church, youth groups, and Bible studies, and *not* why we'd made sure we started each and every day of their lives at home with time in God's Word and prayer.

Well, I want to pass on to you the wisdom my wiser and more seasoned friend gave me. She asked, "Elizabeth, what are you doing to remedy the situation?"

You can be sure when Jim got home that evening, I shared her probing question with him. What *were* we doing to remedy the situation? Nothing! "What *could* we do?" became our passionate prayer concern.

Soon we were led to call Courtney and offer her our credit card number and a gift of $25 each month for books chosen from a Christian book catalog. (And Paul was to select $25 worth of books for himself too!) Just because there were no Christian libraries on Kauai, and just because there were few Christian books in the public libraries, that didn't mean we couldn't help put edifying Christian works into their home and hands and hearts!

And so Courtney began to "feed" on something of substance.

Soon a letter arrived from her telling me that her first selection was a three-pack of biographies on the lives of Fanny Crosby, Dorothy Carey, and Susanna Wesley.

Next a call came saying, "Oh, Mom, I can't wait to discuss Dorothy Carey's life with you!"

Then another note: "Mom, this seems like something you can share with your ladies when you teach." It was an excerpt from a letter written by Susanna Wesley to her son, John, the founder of Methodism:

> I will tell you what rule I observed…when I was young, and too much addicted to childish diversions, which was this—Never to spend more time in mere recreation in one day than I spend in private religious devotions.[1]

Quickly I prayed, "Oh, thank You, Lord! Now *this* is more like it! And thank You too, Lord, for Courtney's encouraging message to me from this wonderful book about a woman who loved You too!"

And after reading the inspiring story of prolific song-writer Fanny Crosby's life, Courtney ordered several volumes on the great hymns of the Christian faith and how they came to be written.

My friend, is there a situation you need to remedy? Are you feeding on foolishness or rooting through ashes or merely sniffing the wind? God—*Jehovah-Rohi*—tells us to beware of the inevitable stumbling and falling that is sure to result. At the same time, He invites us into the safety and shelter of His promised care—the care of *Jehovah-Rohi*, the One who promises to feed and to lead us.

Do you want to be safe from the influence, ways, and lusts of the world and the flesh (1 John 2:16)? From the sin which so easily entangles us (Hebrews 12:1)? Then delight yourself in the Lord, in His provision, in His Word. Faithfully feed on the things that possess true substance and real meaning. When you remember that "all Scripture is given by inspiration by God and is profitable" (2 Timothy 3:16) and partake of such divine substance, then you are fed, you are led, *and* you are safe!

⁓⁓⁓

⁓ More Building Your Confidence Insights ⁓

Just imagine! As one of God's precious sheep you are cherished and cared for by the Good Shepherd! By penning these two Hebrew words—*Jehovah-Rohi*—which translates "the-LORD-is-my-shepherd," David's imagery lifts our thoughts to the highest and tenderest aspect of God's nature. No other name of God carries with it the intimacy and tender friendship of *Jehovah-Rohi*. Yes, you are cared for and cherished—so much so that God promises to lead you and feed you always.

Think of it! The Lord is your Shepherd…and He will take care of you. It's His promise to you!

⚘

When fear regarding the cares of this world
sets in, remember
God's promise to care for you.

2

God Will Always Provide

I shall not want.

PSALM 23:1

And my God shall supply all your need according to His riches in glory by Christ Jesus.

PHILIPPIANS 4:19

*P*erhaps you remember Y2K, the catchphrase that was coined to mark our entry into the twenty-first century, into the year 2000. Originally meant to serve as an advance warning to prepare computers and business systems for new dating, one of Y2K's side effects was rising fear around the globe.

Normally level-headed people sold off their stocks.

General purchases dropped as folks curtailed spending...while gun sales rose.

Even Christians (who have the Lord, *Jehovah-Rohi,* as their Shepherd) stockpiled food, hoarded cash, stored food and water in basements, cancelled Christmas, postponed important decisions, and refused to make commitments into the year 2000.

And Christian book sales on subjects such as prayer and the promises of God were up.[1]

People definitely geared up for hardship.

Hardship, however, is not unique to a new millennium. Hardship has touched mankind throughout time. The Bible and history books are filled with records of economic depressions, social oppressions, wars, famines, and disasters. Suffering has been a fact of life since Adam and Eve disobeyed God (Genesis 3). And because of these realities, it's easy to understand why we're so tempted to look through the corridors of the times to come and succumb to anxiety, worry, fear, and hopelessness. We just don't see how we're going to make it.

But, dear one, our wonderful God has already seen through the corridors of time-future…*and* time-eternal. (Indeed, they are *His* corridors!) He already knows His full-scale plan for mankind. And He already knows His personal plan for you and for each of His children. You see, He alone is the one who knows the end from the beginning (Isaiah 46:10).

When David, the king and sweet singer of Israel, penned Psalm 23, a song of praise about God, about our amazing Shepherd, he wrote…

The Lord is my shepherd; I shall not want.

We learned in the last chapter that "the Lord is my shepherd" is actually a name of God: *Jehovah-Rohi*. But God has other names. And the fact that David could say "I shall not want" reminds me of yet another name of God—*Jehovah-Jireh*—and another characteristic of God for us: His provision.

When these two aspects of God's character—*Jehovah-Rohi* and *Jehovah-Jireh*—are put together, they convey oh so clearly that God leads us, cares for us, *and* He provides for us. Where God guides, He provides. Therefore, we shall not want…for anything!

Meet Jehovah-Jireh

What does *Jehovah-Jireh* mean…and mean to you and me? Most of the compound names of God spring from a specific historic incident, and we first meet *Jehovah-Jireh* in Genesis 22. He is providing for His faithful servant, the biblical patriarch Abraham, and Abraham's son Isaac. Let's watch the scene unfold.

Abraham's command came out of heaven from God: "Take now your son, your only son Isaac, whom you love, and go to the land of Moriah, and offer him there as a burnt offering" (verses 1-2).

Abraham's response was immediate obedience: "So Abraham rose early in the morning…and took…Isaac his son…and went to the place of which God had told him" (verse 3), a place that was about a 60-mile trek.

Abraham's son Isaac had a question: As they walked along with the wood, the fire, and the knife necessary to slay an animal sacrifice, Isaac asked, "Where is the lamb for a burnt offering?" (verse 7).

Abraham's answer revealed his trust in the Lord: "My son, God will provide [*Jehovah-Jireh*] for Himself the lamb for a burnt offering" (verse 8).

Exactly how did *Jehovah-Jireh* provide? Arriving at the place of sacrifice, faithful (and trembling?) Abraham bound Isaac with rope, laid him on an altar, and took out his knife to kill his only son. As Abraham prepared to follow through on God's command to offer his son as a sacrifice, the Angel of the Lord called out from heaven, "Do not lay your hand on the lad, or do anything to him; for now I know that you fear God, since you have not withheld your son, your only son, from Me" (verse 12).

And do you know what happened next? God, *Jehovah-Jireh*,

provided a lamb for the sacrifice. As Abraham looked up, he spotted a ram caught in the bushes, a ram he used in Isaac's place for the burnt offering.

No wonder Abraham named the place The-Lord-Will-Provide! "In the Mount of the LORD it shall be provided" (verse 14).

⟿ Building Your Confidence in Him ⟿

Do you ever feel overwhelmed by something you've been asked to do or something that is expected of you…and you just can't see *how* you can do it? So many of the women I talk to feel overcome by their roles (wife, mother, daughter, grandmother), their responsibilities (at home, in the neighborhood, at school, at church, and on the job), and the challenge of keeping up their health and personal grooming.

Abraham shows us the way. He responded immediately to the call of God. He moved out in obedience, and He trusted the Lord. And…on the other side of his faith, his responding-moving-out-and-trusting actions, was God's provision.

That's how it must be with us too. We have our "commands" (our responsibilities), spelled out in God's Word. And we need to prioritize and plan and prepare and pray about the wisest ways to follow through and fulfill God's commands.

Then the moment comes when we must move out. Action must be taken, whether we think we can "make it" or not. Whether what God is asking of us makes sense or not. Whether it seems doable or not. Whether it feels good or not.

Faith must finally take a step!

- ﹌ The Red Sea didn't part until Moses lifted his hand and his rod (Exodus 14:16,21).

- ﹌ The waters of the Jordan didn't divide until the priests stepped into them (Joshua 3:13).

- ﹌ Rahab's family wasn't saved until she tied a scarlet thread in her window (Joshua 2:21).

- ﹌ The widow's oil didn't increase until she poured it out (2 Kings 4:5).

- ﹌ Naaman's leprosy wasn't cured until he washed in the Jordan River (2 Kings 5:14).

In every one of these situations (and there are many more in the Bible) the miracle occurred *after* faith acted. And in every case the predicament was impossible... absurd. And in every case God pressed His dear children right up to the edge...until common sense and reason had to be abandoned and faith was forced to bloom, until the "seen" had to be replaced with faith that is "unseen."

So, my friend, step up to your impossible situation...and step out in faith. Determine to do what God is asking of you...and act on His command. Then you will know God's provision.

﹌

God Provides

Jehovah-Jireh. How reassuring to know that God sees our needs and provides for them. But how do we know for certain God will provide? We have the *promise* of God (which requires it), but we also have the very nature of the *Person* of God (which demands compliance). He is all-knowing. He is all-wise. He is all-powerful.[3] With God, to see is also to provide. Or, put another way,

> In His omniscience (His complete knowledge),
> God *knows* (or sees) our need;
> In His power, He *can* provide; and
> In His goodness, He *must* provide for what
> His knowledge and wisdom reveal to be
> the true needs of His people.

Think a little further. For God to see a need in His child and *not* meet that need would be evil, and God, by His very nature, cannot be evil or be tempted by evil (James 1:13). Therefore, with God, pre-vision and pro-vision are one and the same. When His pre-vision sees a need, His pro-vision meets it!

⚬ Building Your Confidence in Him ⚬

I just paused to make a list of life's needs, and I came up with a needs list that I believe fits for most of us.

First and foremost, there's the physical area of everyday life, the need you and I have for food and clothing and shelter. And yet we know God's Word tells us not to worry about our lives—about what we'll eat or drink or wear (Matthew 6:25). Why? Because God feeds the birds of the air, and He'll also feed us (verse 26). And God clothes the lilies of the field, and He'll also clothe us (verse 28).

The Bible also describes God's amazing (and miraculous!) provision for the Israelites as they wandered for 40 years in the wilderness. As the people in Nehemiah's day affirmed,

> You also gave Your good Spirit to instruct them, and did not withhold Your manna from their mouth, and gave them water for their thirst. Forty years You sustained them in the wilderness, so that they lacked nothing: Their clothes did not wear out and their feet did not swell (Nehemiah 9:20-21).

God, *Jehovah-Jireh,* provided guidance, food, water, clothes, and health for His people—all they needed—and He did it for 40 years! Now, *that's* provision! And, marvel of marvels, "they lacked nothing" (which is the same picture we have in Psalm 23:1: *"I shall not want"*). That's our God, *Jehovah-Jireh!*

Then there's our need for the less measurable things of life—for leadership, for comfort, for instruction, for encouragement, for protection, for love, for safety, for purpose, for belonging and fellowship and friendship. What a sweet thought to realize we can count on *Jehovah-Jireh's* promise to provide for them too!

Later, in Psalm 23, you'll see God meet each and every one of life's requirements, but for now enjoy these reflections about God's provision from Dr. Harry Ironside, former pastor of Moody Memorial Church in Chicago. He wrote of God and His promises,

> I shall not want...
>
> ...rest, for He maketh me to lie down.

...refreshment, for He leadeth me
    beside the still waters.

...restoration, for He restoreth my
    soul.

...guidance, for He leadeth me in the
    paths of righteousness.

...confidence, for I will fear no evil.

...companionship, for Thou art with
    me.

...comfort, for Thy rod and Thy staff,
    they comfort me.

...provision, for Thou preparest a
    table.

...joy, for my cup runneth over.

...anything in this life, for goodness
    and mercy shall follow me all the
    days of my life

...anything in eternity, for I will dwell
    in the house of the Lord forever.[2]

"I shall not want." These words of promise, dear
one, should translate in your heart and mind to "I shall
not fear!" Truly, God promises to provide your every
need, present and future!

⚜

God's Provision Is Seen

Here's one more thought as we consider God's provision. Do you
remember how Abraham answered Isaac's question regarding the

lamb for the sacrifice? He said, "My son, God will provide [*Jehovah-Jireh*] for Himself the lamb for a burnt offering" (Genesis 22:8). This is the same as Abraham's saying "God's provision shall be seen" (verse 14).

And it was! Right there on Mount Moriah, the place where God instructed Abraham to sacrifice his son, *Jehovah-Jireh's* provision was seen in the ram caught in the bushes. As the Living Bible translates Genesis 22:14, "God will see to it."[3]

What a wonderful wealth we have in the character of God! As this title *Jehovah-Jireh* denotes, our loving Shepherd *sees* our needs and *sees to* our needs. And when we *see* His provision, we need to *see to it* that He is greatly praised!

~ *Building Your Confidence in Him* ~

Before you leave this marvelous revelation about our marvelous God, cherish the fullness of the meaning of *Jehovah-Jireh* as revealed in these translations of Psalm 23:1, "The LORD is my Shepherd, I shall not want":

The LORD is my shepherd, therefore, I can lack nothing.

The LORD shepherds me, I shall never be in need.

Yahweh is my shepherd, I lack nothing.

The LORD takes care of me as His sheep; I will not be without any good thing.

Because the LORD is my shepherd, I have everything I need![4]

The promises of Psalm 23, verse 1, are life-changing!

We need to deeply embed them into our souls and evidence strong faith and confidence by counting on God's promised provision for our every need...forever. Praise His name!

∼∿∼

What famous British preacher G. Campbell Morgan wrote of Psalm 23:1 is true: "This is not only the first statement of this song, it is its inclusive statement. Everything that follows [verse 1] interprets the glory and sufficiency of the fact [here] declared. When this is said... the LORD is my shepherd, I shall not want...all is said."[5]

———— ∿ ————

Step up to your impossible situation...
and step out in faith.
God leads you and cares for you
and will provide for you!
Where God guides, He provides.
Therefore, you shall not want for anything.

———— ∿ ————

3

God Gives You Rest

He makes me to lie down in green pastures.

PSALM 23:2

Come to Me, all you who labor and are heavy laden,
and I will give you rest.
Take My yoke upon you and learn from Me,
for I am gentle and lowly in heart,
and you will find rest for your souls.

MATTHEW 11:28-29

his can't be Los Angeles!"

As I turned my car off the busy state highway in Simi Valley, California, and onto a narrow asphalt road lined for miles on both sides with graceful five-story-high eucalyptus trees set ten feet apart, I was amazed. Quickly civilization had disappeared, and I was alone in the beautiful, untouched foothills of the Santa Monica mountains. Eventually the rural drive led me to the old stone gatehouse of The Brandeis Institute, where I had a job interview. I rang a bell and waited. Finally the estate keeper arrived to open the gate and let me through. After another half-mile drive, I arrived at the century-old stone hunting lodge that housed the offices of the Institute.

I felt like I was back in time...or was I in another country? I couldn't tell. But I liked what I saw and smelled and sensed. I could feel myself relaxing even as I faced the stress of an interview. Tucked away from hectic freeways, tract homes, and strip malls, the quiet pastoral beauty of this undisturbed hill country was wonderfully peaceful.

Later, after I began working at the Institute, I learned the history of this restful place from the Israeli director, Dr. Shlomo Bardin. The Jewish community of Los Angeles had specifically selected this country site because it reminded them of their homeland in Israel. Its tranquil hills looked like those in the Judean hills of the Holy Land. The mountains, the climate, and the vegetation were similar too. And so The Brandeis Institute was founded on this remote acreage, a kibbutz-style retreat center was built, and the land was left unchanged. To this wonderful "home away from home" Jews came each Friday afternoon before sunset to withdraw from the mainstream, to reflect on their heritage, to worship, and to rest.

The last day of my work week was short because of the Jewish Shabbat. I have to admit that each Friday when I got off work, before their worship began, I wished that I too could stay and rest in this picturesque setting.

Ahhh, rest! Our bodies need it, and our souls crave it. And now, as we step into verse 2 of the Shepherd Psalm, we discover that rest is yet another one of God's precious promises to us as His precious sheep: "He makes [us] to lie down in green pastures." Let's see what God has in mind for our rest.

The Place of Rest

First, there's a *place* God guides us to, a place of "green pastures." And what do you suppose is in those green pastures where the Shepherd will ensure that we lie down?

Food. Food is abundantly available in God's green pastures. That's the picture the psalmist is painting with his descriptive language—a picture of abundance and luxury. A good shepherd carefully picks a place of pastureland that's filled to overflowing with fresh, new, tender grass. His heart is set on finding a place containing plenty of delicate green plants that will provide nourishment, health, and fresh energy for his sheep.

Rest. Rest too occurs as the sheep lay down in green pastures. The scene is one of satisfaction and rest. Of calm and contentment. Of sheer enjoyment. Oh, would that grass ever be cool on a hot day in a dry desert climate, providing the perfect place of refreshment and rest for weary sheep.

⟶ Building Your Confidence in Him ⟵

Dear one, as a sheep who belongs to the Great Shepherd, you too can partake of green pastures. How? By having "quiet times" with the Lord. You have the Shepherd and all of His Word available to you if you'll simply lie down in His green pastures and partake! All you need to do is stop everything and enjoy a time of resting and lingering with the Lord as you feed on His Word and thrive on His love.

What happens when you withdraw from the clamor of a sinful world and enter into the serenity available in God's green pastures? You experience the same sense of rejuvenation, the same revival of spirit, the same deep satisfaction that sheep enjoy when resting in the presence of a faithful shepherd they trust.

It's good to check up on yourself about your time in God's Word, in His green pastures:

Necessary—Do you believe that time spent with God in the green pastures of His Word is an absolute necessity, just as food and rest are absolutely necessary for every sheep? J.I. Packer, author of *Knowing God,* warns, "Disregard the study of [the Word] of God and you sentence yourself to stumble and blunder through life, blindfolded, as it were, with no sense of direction, and no understanding of what surrounds you."[1]

Regular—Is your time spent in the lush pastures of God's Word regular? Is it daily? When you think about how regularly and how often you eat physical food, how does your feeding on spiritual food measure up?

One evening, at a roundtable discussion held at our dining table, my husband, Jim, was sharing the tiny pamphlet *Seven Minutes with God* with a group of men who were students at The Master's College, where Jim led a Bible study.[2] Jim had purchased a copy of this priceless booklet for each one of them and was walking them through its seven-minute format for daily devotions. The young men began to squirm, and finally one of them cleared his throat and said what the others were thinking: "But, Professor George, isn't seven minutes a day with God in a quiet time just a little...ah...er...*un*spiritual?"

My wise husband answered this question with a question: "Well, let me ask you men: How many of you spent an hour this past week in devotions?" When very few raised their hands (and while the others looked down sheepishly at theirs!), Jim continued, "You see, seven minutes a day with God is better than no minutes a day with God...and seven minutes a day with God adds up to about an hour a week."

Do you need to begin feeding regularly in God's green pastures? (And always remember: A wee bite is better than no bite at all.)

Increasing—Is your time spent in the lush pastures of the Scriptures increasing? Jim didn't mean that the men in his Bible-study group should *only* spend seven minutes each day with God for the rest of their lives. No, time in God's Word should be ever-increasing.

So do as Ruth Graham said, citing one of her favorite Bible translations: Indulge yourself! Do whatever you have to do to make time in God's Word exciting and meaningful. Keep on willfully indulging yourself…and in larger time increments and frequency.

Which of these stages best describes your recent times in God's Word?

1. *the cod liver oil stage*—you take it like medicine;

2. *the shredded wheat stage*—it's nourishing but dry; or

3. *the peaches and cream stage*—it's consumed with passion and pleasure.[3]

What steps can you take to reach the peaches and cream stage? Oh, how I hope and pray that you (and me too!) have an insatiable appetite for rich fellowship with the Lord through His Word that nothing else will satisfy!

⚓

Aren't you glad that God provides a place—His green pastures—for us to rest in and feed in? But there's more!

The Plan for Rest

In addition to a *place* of rest, we can also rest in God's *plan*. In His wisdom He plans (and ensures!) that we "lie down." Digging a little deeper, I found that the kind of "lying down" the Shepherd has in mind is no nervous pause or quick respite. No, the idea expressed is one of s-t-r-e-t-c-h-i-n-g out, of lying full-out, of completely reclining. The vivid picture is one of enjoyment and contentment and satisfaction. You see, while lying down in this way, total rest occurs. Relaxation and refreshment take place.

I remember reading about Russian writer Alexander Solzhenitsyn's days in a Russian prison. As part of his torture he wasn't allowed to rest or sit down or lie down for days on end. Instead he was worked around the clock. I remember thinking, *Now that would be the worst torture there is—to be utterly exhausted, literally dead on your feet, and unable to lie down, stretch out, rest, and recover.*

But as I studied this beloved and familiar old psalm, I learned a few interesting facts about why a sheep doesn't like to lie down.

Reason #1—Fear. A sheep that is afraid will not lie down and get the rest it needs. In one example I read, a shepherd led his flock to a small brook that had a bounty of grass on both sides. Yet the flock refused to lie down because a large dog was on the other side of the stream.

Even after the shepherd slung a stone and frightened the dog off, the sheep still wouldn't relax. What did it take to persuade the sheep to lie down? It took the shepherd walking ahead of them to the brook. It took the presence of the shepherd to dispel all fear.

⌁ *Building Your Confidence in Him* ⌁

You too have the presence of the Shepherd, dear one. Therefore, as the Scripture says, "Fear not":

- Fear not, for I am with you; be not dismayed, for I am your God. I will strengthen you, yes, I will help you, I will uphold you with My righteous right hand (Isaiah 41:10).

- Do not be afraid, nor be dismayed, for the LORD your God is with you wherever you go (Joshua 1:9).

- Do not fear nor be afraid of them; for the LORD your God, He is the One who goes with you. He will not leave you nor forsake you (Deuteronomy 31:6).

- My Presence will go with you, and I will give you rest" (Exodus 33:14).

With these powerful promises from God to strengthen you, there's hope and help for you to defeat panic and anxiety and to get relief from insomnia. If these are problems for you, memorize these verses…and trust in their promise. Put them to work for you. Then, when you lie down, you can rest in the presence of your loving Shepherd. And when you rise up after rest, declare in chorus with David, "I lay down and slept; I awoke, for the LORD sustained me" (Psalm 3:5).

⌁⚓⌁

Reason #2—Hunger. It's a fact that a sheep that's hungry will not lie down and receive the rest it needs. Instead, it wanders about restlessly, frantically searching for food. Thus the discontented sheep adds lack of rest to its problem of lack of food. It soon loses its vigor and vitality, failing to thrive.

But, beloved, our Good Shepherd feeds His sheep. As *Jehovah-Jireh* ("I shall not want"), He makes sure our food is always available. All we have to do is decide to feed upon it...and indulge to our heart's content!

⤳ Building Your Confidence in Him ⤳

My pastor's wife, knowing I was teaching Psalm 23, hand-carried a valuable volume on shepherding all the way back from New Zealand to California just for me. She'd met the widow of the author, who had been a shepherd, in the green, rolling hills of lush New Zealand. In his book, he shared this insight:

> So many Christians attempt to satisfy their hunger...from an occasional few minutes' "feeding" from the pulpit, from a radio broadcast, or from a television message, while others seek to satisfy their needs from the odd old devotional book, or the occasional Christian programme. This is not enough...to sustain the needy soul on a daily basis...God provides for us on a daily basis, but we must plan to partake of His provision on a daily basis.[4]

Are you following the Shepherd? Are you lying

down in His green pastures? And are you feeding to
your heart's content on His provision?

⚞

Reason #3—Fighting. A sheep that's involved in or even wit-
nessing fighting also won't lie down and receive the rest it needs.
Battles between members of a flock rob all the sheep of the rest
they need because, when any tension or uneasiness exists, the flock
will refuse to lie down, relax, and rest.

⚞ Building Your Confidence in Him ⚞

Many Christians are weary and worn, not because
of intense conflict with the evil one, but because of
arguments among themselves. It's frightening to realize
the harm done to others when we argue and fight in
our homes and in our churches.

The chief challenge to us is to be sure we're not par-
ticipating in this kind of fighting. You and I must take
care that we're not a source of tension for others.

And one more thing. We can enjoy rest when we
withdraw from the friction and the fodder of gossip produced by others. Why feed on such slop when we can
feed on the beauty of the Lord and enjoy His holiness?
As His devoted sheep, look to Him (and not to "them")
and go about the business of your grand duty and your
chief work of confidently following the Shepherd.

⚞

The Procedure for Rest

So let's see now...

We have a *place* to sup with the Shepherd (His *green pastures*).

We have a *plan* for ensuring that we sup with Him (that we *lie down*).

And now we learn that our Lord has a *procedure* that guarantees our time with Him—He *makes* us lie down...even when we don't want to!

God's procedure of *making* us lie down is a call to trust Him. Why? Because He alone knows the future. Only He knows what lies ahead for us. What's around the next bend...over the next hill...on the other side of the green pasture. Will it be a long, steep climb? Will the path narrow as it leads us around a dangerous mountain? Will the trail take us into the valley of the shadow of death? Are we headed into a desert or a roaring storm?

The Shepherd knows our path. And He also knows His sheep and what it takes to prepare us for the journey. And so the Shepherd *makes* us lie down to fortify us for the trek. He makes certain we won't tire, that we're not at risk because of weariness, that we're invigorated from our pasture-time for any strenuous climb. With His eye on tomorrow, He leads us today.

Do you know the results of our time spent in the hush of communion with the Shepherd and apart from the rush of the commonplace? As God's prophet Isaiah reports, "Those who wait on the LORD shall renew their strength; they shall mount up with wings like eagles, they shall run and not be weary, they shall walk and not faint" (Isaiah 40:31). Our Shepherd knows this. And so all along life's way, He *makes* us lie down in green pastures.

⚘ Building Your Confidence in Him ⚘

As I reflected on God's procedure of *making* us lie down in His green pastures, I thought of a number of ways He accomplishes our rest. Illness, surgery, and convalescence afford us time with the Shepherd. So do pregnancy and childbirth. And exhaustion too certainly places us in the grassy pastures of the Lord.

Still another category of time in God's pastures involves plain ol' being passed over, being overlooked for service and ministry. I experienced a time like that when my family spent time in Singapore as missionaries.

Why did our church choose to send my husband to serve in Singapore? Well, one very practical reason was Singapore's Changi Airport, which serves every Asian country. The plane carrying our little family of four had barely landed and we disembarked before my Jim was back in the air, off to another country. In essence, Jim's ministry "took off" before we landed! He was invited to preach, to speak, to minister not only in the churches in Singapore, but also in neighboring countries.

And me? I sat...and sat...and sat some more. My phone was definitely *not* ringing. "Why, Lord?" I prayed. "Why did I spend these past months preparing to serve You here? Why did I so carefully select resources and topics and teaching notes and messages for a ministry to women here?" On and on my "whys" for the Lord went.

Of course God knew what was happening! I can tell you *now* why my phone was amazingly silent. My all-knowing, all-wise Shepherd was making me lie down in green pastures. It was an enforced rest—one that accomplished much in the three months no one called, when I had no outreach ministry. My primary job was to help my family adjust to a new culture…to adjust to living in a climate near the equator…to adjust to a life of walking and buses and taxis—and no car.

I needed time to set up a home for my family… to learn to shop daily in the Asian food markets…to prepare mysterious foods in unusual (to me!) ways.

My daughters Katherine and Courtney, then in sixth and fifth grades, needed time to transition into a new school setting.

And so we waited. Or rather, *I* waited.

Looking back to my three months of pasture-time in Singapore, I thank God for *making* me rest from ministry as He supplied what my dear family needed. They needed me, they needed a home, and they needed an anchor of stability (me again!).

One other rarity that God gave me in that precious period of time was solitude. He gave me months of "quiet time" with Him. My empty calendar and silent phone and lack of friends opened up hours on end each and every day…to spend with Him.

Waiting. Waiting is hard for us in today's instant-access society. But what happens, dear one, while you and I wait on the Lord in His green pastures?

> ⚓ *Waiting* creates an opportunity to learn to trust the Lord. We are forced to come to grips with the fact that He alone knows what He is doing.

> ⚓ *Waiting* causes us to grow in patience as we

wait…and wait…and wait some more…until
finally we are content just to be with the Lord.

⚬ *Waiting* in the presence of God encourages
us to know Him in new ways as "waiting
time" forces creative fellowship to occur.

⚬ *Waiting* energizes us for the walk (or race or
battle!) ahead. God's prophet Elijah lay down
in His green pastures and slept and ate and
drank—and then went on in the strength of
that pasture-time for 40 days and 40 nights
(1 Kings 19:4-8).

Are you waiting, my friend? It will be helpful if you
think of your waiting time as being like a ship in a lock.
It's not that you *wouldn't* like to go forward—you just
can't. Why? Forward movement is impossible in the
lock, but *while* you're there…*while* you're unable to
move ahead…you're moving up, up, up instead as the
water floods in and raises the ship. It's the same for us.
A time of waiting "locks" us into a life of study, a life
of prayer, a life of lingering with the Shepherd, a life of
preparation…until we rise up and move ahead again,
having received from our time of rest all we need for
life's next challenge.

So welcome waiting! No matter how it looks or
feels, your waiting times are God's green pastures—
pastures for food, for coolness, for rest, for relaxation,
for health, for preparation, for revival, for intimacy
with your Lord.

⚬⚬⚬

Aren't you glad God has a *place* for you to rest, a *plan* for your rest, and a *procedure* that ensures you do rest? As a variety of translations of this wonderful promise, when woven together, assure us, "He makes me lie down in green pastures—where He creates a resting-place for me to repose in, and there He shall feed me until I am satisfied."[5]

---

*What happens when you withdraw from the clamor
of a sinful world and enter into the serenity
available in God's green pastures?
You experience the same sense of rejuvenation,
the same revival of spirit, the same deep satisfaction
that literal sheep enjoy when resting in
the presence of a faithful shepherd.*

4

God's Peace Is Always Available to You

He leads me beside the still waters.

Peace I leave with you, My peace I give to you;
not as the world gives do I give to you.
Let not your heart be troubled, neither let it be afraid.

JOHN 14:27

Like a river glorious, is God's perfect peace...
Not a surge of worry, not a shade of care,
not a blast of hurry touch the spirit there.
Stayed upon Jehovah, hearts are fully blest
finding, as He promised, perfect peace and rest.[1]

FRANCES R. HAVERGAL

o you have a favorite place? A special place that ministers to your soul? That sharpens your perspective? That stimulates you in fresh new ways? Jim and I have found just such a place where we love to retreat. One of the best features about "our place" is that we don't have to travel very far to reach it. It's just a pleasant 45-minute drive from our home.

What's there that regularly draws us? Well, there's the expanse of the Pacific Ocean and its never-ceasing, ever-ebbing-and-flowing surf. We never fail to walk along its sandy shore.

After our walk on the beach, there's a charming sidewalk café beside a large pool that's fed by the spill of a soothing waterfall where we like to share a snack. There's also a cascading fountain in the center of the veranda where we enjoy our sandwich and coffee.

One day while I was thinking about our place (actually yearning for another visit there...*soon!*), it struck me that *water* is the common denominator in all that Jim and I love to do and see there. Yes, it's the water that lures us there. And once we're there, it calms us, inspires us, energizes us, and moves us to focus on God's larger plans for us.

As we look at yet another of God's many provisions for us as His dear sheep, we discover an image of water. And beside it, beloved, God promises we will find the much-yearned-for and much-needed peace of mind and heart we so long for as "He leads [us] beside the still waters" (Psalm 23:2).

The Still Waters

Let's imagine that you were asked to fill out a survey. One of the questions is "What causes you to seek peace?" How would you answer? As I was preparing for this chapter, I went through this exercise. Here are some of the answers I came up with. Do any of them match up with yours?

Busyness is #1 on my list. I do a lot of running here and there. There's always one more errand to run, one more minute needed in the kitchen, one more meal to fix, one more load of laundry to do, one more phone call to make, one more...On and on my to-do list goes.

Responsibility is next. You know, all those duties that fall on our feminine shoulders? And the expectation—from ourselves and from others—that the items on our to-do list will be performed. These demands can become a heavy burden.

Tension showed up next on my list. Whenever something is wrong in a home or a relationship, the tension and uneasiness drain us.

Noise too made my list. The noise of clamoring. The noise of too many people and too much traffic. The noise of neighbors. The noise of people arguing, yelling, reacting in anger.

I'm sure you can think of many more situations that would leave us both craving a moment of peace. But good news awaits us right here in verse two of Psalm 23: "He leads me beside the still waters."

He—the Shepherd—knows all about our need for peace and provides it. He made us, He planned our path, He knows our every challenge, and He provides the peace we need for fulfilling His will for our lives.

Leads—Our Shepherd most definitely leads us to the places where peace is plentiful, and He makes sure we attain it.

Still waters—He leads us beside still, restful waters of comfort. The last thing you and I need when we're on the edge of collapse is the threatening power of raging waters and thundering rapids. The Shepherd knows this too. He wisely leads us to a peaceful place beside a quiet, tranquil stream.

We know that our souls become dry on a steady diet of stress. We quickly become depleted and weary. We stagger, we stumble, we crumble, and we make errors in judgment...all because we need time beside the still waters. Take heart, beloved! *Our God leads us beside the still waters.*

∼Building Your Confidence in Him∼

Have you visited the still waters of God's peace and comfort lately? The waters are there...waiting for you. And the Shepherd is there too. Refreshment is there. Revival is there. Renewal is there. Comfort is there. And peace is there too.

God gives you His peace, and He extends rest to the weary and renewal to the exhausted. He wants your soul to be at peace, and He promises to accomplish that. Drink deeply of Him from His Word! Partake often. Commune with Him in prayer beside His peaceful waters. Allow Him to lead you there now. Make God's still waters "your place."

∼⦇⦈∼

Oh, the beauty of Psalm 23:2! "He leads me beside the still waters." Here the peace that makes us whole and places us in harmony with God is characterized by cool, fresh water. By the still waters, the rest of peace is enjoyed. As verse 2 has been translated, "My spirit was lifted and my endurance renewed."

Meet Jehovah-Shalom, the God of Peace

This seems like a good time to look at another characteristic and name of God that's illustrated in Psalm 23. God's promise in verse 2 to give us His peace points us to *Jehovah-Shalom,* meaning "Jehovah, my peace" or "Jehovah brings peace." And just as we've seen with the other names that portray God's character—*Jehovah-Rohi* and *Jehovah-Jireh*—this name is derived from God's dealings with His people.

We first meet *Jehovah-Shalom* in the book of Judges when the reigning judge, Gideon, "built an altar...to the LORD, and called it The-LORD-Shalom," which means "Jehovah is peace" (6:24). God's people were involved in a repeated cycle of sin at this time in their history. Things got worse and worse as God's people forgot Jehovah, their God. Instead, they were turning to the gods of the people around them. Truly it was a time when "everyone did what was right in his own eyes" (Judges 21:25)! God's people corrupted themselves with idolatries and abominations. As a result, they lost their purity, prosperity, freedom, and peace.

Down, down went God's chosen people, the apple of His eye. Soon a desperate pattern of sin–punishment–repentance–deliverance emerged. It was a dark, dark, dark time for the Israelites, a time of alternating prosperity and adversity, of repenting and sinning, of deliverance and slavery. There was definitely no peace in their roller-coaster existence.

Meet Gideon, the Judge

Enter Gideon, the fifth judge appointed by God to lead and deliver His people. We first meet Gideon in his own dark place, hiding in a winepress for fear of the Midianites, the enemies of the Israelites. Gideon had scraped together a scant handful of wheat the enemy hadn't destroyed and was secretly threshing it (Judges 6:11). Into this dark scene in this dark time in the history of the children of God, the Angel of Jehovah suddenly, brilliantly, and wondrously appeared. The angel promised deliverance for God's people and called Gideon to lead them.

Poor Gideon! He doubted. He hesitated. He questioned. He wondered. He squirmed. He feared. But the Lord led Gideon to the still waters and stilled his fears with these comforting words: "Peace be with you; do not fear, you shall not die" (6:23).

Then Gideon worshiped. (Wouldn't you!) He built an altar to the Lord and named it *Jehovah-Shalom,* meaning "The Altar of Peace with Jehovah" (6:24). This wonderful label signified Gideon's confident anticipation of God's promise of victory and the long-awaited and much-needed peace.

⭢ *Building Your Confidence in Him* ⭢

I certainly don't want to dwell on negatives, but we can learn from the Israelites here. The lack of peace they experienced clearly shows us the importance of obedience in our quest to know God's peace.

Is your daily life characterized by trouble, chaos, and disaster? Do you feel like you're living under the pile, always behind, making little or no progress? That things are always out of control or never quite in order? Does your life lack the mark of God's peace? Is there an absence of *Jehovah-Shalom?*

Events and crises will and do disrupt the peaceful pattern of life. But it's also true that we know in our heart of hearts when things are not right between us and the Lord. We know when our wandering ways are resulting in turmoil. Yes, we definitely know when we are failing in our love and obedience to Jehovah.

As Psalm 23, verse 3, guarantees, *our loving Shepherd leads.* But we must heed. He leads, but we must follow. Here are some insightful comments:

- ⭢ "Loving the LORD is not an emotional goosebump; it is a commitment to selfless obedience" (John MacArthur).

- ⭢ "Our part is to trust God fully, to obey Him implicitly, and to follow His instructions faithfully" (V. Raymond Edman).

- ⭢ "To know God is to experience His love in Christ, and to return that love in obedience" (C.H. Dodd).

⭢⭢⭢

~*More Building Your Confidence in Him*~

There's another kind of following that has nothing to do with disobedience and everything to do with commitment. This was Gideon's situation. Fear and doubt caused him to hesitate in his commitment to the Lord. And the result was a definite lack of peace in his life. And, my friend, fear and doubt affect women just like you and me too. Let me explain.

One year I met a lady in the Pacific Northwest who was struggling with commitment. On a break during a seminar I was giving, this dear woman poured out her problem to me. There were no blatant sins in her life. There were no glaring areas of disobedience. There was no stubborn refusal to follow the Lord. There was simply a personal and serious life challenge. And her refusal to take the challenge was causing this lady obvious turmoil.

The challenge was born the day this precious sister in Christ went with her husband to a missions conference. It was a thrilling time for both of them. At the end of the conference each person was given a three-by-five card with simple words on it:

Anything
Anywhere
Any time
At any cost

_____   _____
Date   Signature

The speaker at the gathering was asking each person to prayerfully sign and date the card with the four A's.

"Honey, can I borrow your pen?" my friend's husband whispered immediately. As she handed him her pen, she noticed that he could hardly wait to sign away! It was no problem for *him*.

Oh, but in *her* heart the struggle raged. *Anything? Anywhere? Any time? At any cost?* No, she just couldn't sign. She had to pray. Truly, the challenge pierced deeply...to her very soul...and her spirit was in upheaval.

But the story doesn't end here. Nearly five years later, at another women's conference in Washington, guess who walked up to me during the break? This friend who had struggled so. This time she finished her story. She glowed as she shared that after seven months—*seven months!*—of prayer and agonizing and fitful heart-searching, she finally signed her card. In fact, it was a treasure she carried in her Bible and pulled out to show to me.

Will you join with this dear saint (and her husband!) in following God's leading? Will you sign the four A's? Will you sing along with the hymn writer: "Where He leads me I will follow...I'll go with Him, with Him all the way"?[2] (And, we might add, *anywhere, any time,* and *at any cost!*)

God's role is to lead. Yours is to follow.

So, how are you doing in the Following Department? Have you looked fully into the Shepherd's wonderful face and into His eyes of love and whispered, "Truly, dear Lord, where You lead me, I will follow"? Do these words express the deep sentiment of your heart? Are you following Him? If so, you are truly enjoying God's promise of peace.

⚊⚊

Meet Gideon, the Warrior

Let's get back to Gideon and get the full story. As you remember, when we met him he was hiding, trying to thresh out some grain for food without being seen by his enemies (Judges 6:11). That's when the Angel of the Lord appeared...

> ...with a proclamation: "You shall save Israel from the hand of the Midianites" (verse 14).

> ...with a promise: "Surely I will be with you, and you shall defeat the Midianites" (verse 16).

> ...with peace: "Peace be with you; do not fear" (verse 23).

> ...with power: "The LORD is with you, you mighty man of valor!" (verse 12).

And the result? These assurances and gifts from God transformed Gideon from being fearful to being a fearless leader of God's people. As the fifth judge in Israel, Gideon acted with confidence, defeated the Midianite army, excelled as a military strategist, was offered the title of king, and was inducted into God's "Hall of Faith" found in Hebrews 11.

⤳ *Building Your Confidence in Him* ⤳

Do you remember Gideon's initial responses to God's call to service? They included doubt…hesitation…questioning…wondering…squirming…and fear. These are certainly not responses that suggest peace of mind! Unfortunately they are responses that sometimes define you and me as we go through life. Do any of these words currently describe your walk with God? Is He leading the hesitant, reticent sheep in you? Is He trying to use you in mighty ways for His purposes…but you're hemming and hawing, dawdling and fidgeting, fussing and fuming, stewing and worrying?

We fail to have peace when we forget (like Gideon did) that God never asks for *us* to have confidence in ourselves. He only asks that we have confidence in *Him*. When God commands, God supplies.

And what did God supply to Gideon so that He could valiantly fulfill God's command? The strength he needed. Gideon was a simple farmer, but when enabled and strengthened by God, this man was transformed into a mighty warrior, a mighty man of valor, a man of mighty faith, a confident follower of God

The same transformation is possible for you. Your obedience—a true mark of our faith—allows God to transform the meek into the mighty. He will do the transforming—that's His role. But you must do the yielding—that's your role.

Are you trusting in the Lord? Are you allowing Him who is mighty to do great things in…and through… and for…you? God promises you'll not only know His peace as you look to His promises, but you'll also know His power!

Meet the Prince of Peace

Before we finish verse 2 and our visit to the still waters, let's behold the Prince of Peace. To enjoy peace and harmony with God means to enjoy the harmony of a close, intimate relationship with Him. And it is Jesus Christ, the Prince of Peace (Isaiah 9:6), who makes this type of relationship with God possible. Peace with God includes...

> ... *harmony*—to be in harmony with God due to the payment of a debt.

> ... *a peace offering*—restored fellowship between God and mankind, accomplished by Jesus' shed blood (see the peace offering of Leviticus 3).

Dear one, Jesus, the Prince of Peace, satisfies both of these definitions of peace.

⏤ Building Your Confidence in Him ⏤

And now it's time for the most important reflection you'll spend in this book. Do you truly belong to Christ? Are you truly in the family of God? Are you a Christian who enjoys the peace of God and the God of peace? Are you a child of God? Have you been reconciled to God through His Son, Jesus Christ? Are your sins washed white as snow by the shed blood of Jesus? Is He your Savior, your Shepherd of Peace?

Just to be sure the path to God is absolutely clear to you, prayerfully consider these facts:

> ⮑ *The fact of sin*—Romans 3:23 states, "All have sinned and fall short of the glory of God."

> ⮑ *The fact of judgment*—Romans 6:23 teaches

us that "the wages of sin is death, but the gift of God is eternal life in Christ Jesus our Lord."

⤳ *The fact of Christ's death for sins*—Romans 5:8 tells us that "God demonstrates His own love toward us, in that while we were still sinners, Christ died for us."

⤳ *The fact of acceptance of Christ by faith*— Romans 10:9 shows us the way: "If you confess with your mouth the Lord Jesus and believe in your heart that God has raised Him from the dead, you will be saved."

⤳ *The fact of peace*—Romans 5:1 tells us that "having been justified by faith, we have peace with God through our Lord Jesus Christ."

If you're not yet God's child, make this your time of accepting Christ by faith. Your peace will begin immediately, and so will your confidence. If you're already a child of God, spend this time of reflection thanking and praising Him for the peace He extends to you through His Son Jesus.

⤳⤳⤳

⟿ A Prayer for Peace ⟿

And now, dear Lord, I acknowledge afresh that You are the God of all peace, my Jehovah-Shalom. You offer me Your peace. My job is to receive. You give me Your peace. My job is to take it. You lead me to Your still waters. My role is to follow. You extend Your hand. My role is to take hold. May I enjoy Your presence and the tranquility of the still waters where You pour out your promise of peace. Amen.

God, who gives you His peace, extends rest to the weary and renewal to the exhausted. He wants your soul to be at peace, and He promises to accomplish that peace.

5

God Is Your Healer

He restores my soul.

PSALM 23:3

Praise the LORD!...
He heals the brokenhearted and
binds up their wounds.

PSALM 147:1,3

*B*ecause Jim and I are active in ministry, it seems like we know more than our share of widows. We've been through the season of widowhood with Jim's dear mother twice. And we've walked through the valley of the shadow of death with many of the dear ladies in the seniors' class Jim once pastored...emerging with them on the other side when they stepped out of that dark valley without a partner. Some of the women's losses were tragic, announced simply and finally by a ring of the telephone and a voice bearing the awful news of loss. Others suffered daily as they watched their beloved husbands linger through cancer or decline. Both extremes—and everything in between—were hard to handle.

We know that death for any of God's children is an ultimate

victory and precious in His sight (Psalm 116:15). But, still, the loss of a loved one is painful for the one left behind, for the one who must go on walking with the Shepherd alone, pressed into yet another new life season.

And certainly, there are other hardships in life that are devastating. Disability. The physical suffering of surgery, cancer, illness, an accident. The collapse of the family. Rejection. Disappointment. Betrayal. Calamity. The list can go on and so...and so must life.

But how? *How* are we to go on? *How* are we to cope with these sapping certainties of life? And *what* are you and I to do to handle life after a life-altering incident? God once again comes to our rescue! In our times of pain and sorrow, God's tender care goes into action with His promise to heal us. As the psalmist's next four words so beautifully state, "He restores my soul" (verse 3).

Looking back for a moment at what we've learned about what it means to be one of the Great Shepherd's sheep, our conclusions are staggering:

- ⤳ We have the promise of His care and provision (verse 1).
- ⤳ We have the promise of His rest and peace (verse 2).
- ⤳ We have the promise of His healing restoration (verse 3).

Our wonderful Shepherd not only takes care of our physical requirements, but He also sees to our spiritual needs. He ministers to the spirit and soul as well as the physical body. God's abundant provision revives us physically, but in this present promise—"He restores my soul"—we witness the Lord healing us spiritually.

The Character of Jehovah-Rophe

There's another name of God that fits as we're discussing the promise of God's healing restoration—the name *Jehovah-Rophe* (pronounced ro-fáy). This wondrous name means "the LORD heals," and there's a remarkable history behind it. Here's what happened.

After God's people were released from their bondage in Egypt and delivered from Pharaoh's army at the Red Sea, they journeyed into new territory. Jubilant and still marveling over God's many miracles on their behalf, the Israelites stepped into their dream future...only to find there was no water to drink. Water was finally discovered at Marah, but it was bitter and undrinkable (Exodus 15).

Then Moses, who had been a shepherd for 40 years, remembered the One who takes care of His sheep. He cried out for help to the Lord...and was answered. Jehovah showed Moses a tree, which, when cast into the bitter water, instantly made it sweet. Jehovah provided, announcing, "For I am the LORD who heals you" (Exodus 15:26).

What an object lesson this encounter with *Jehovah-Rophe,* the Lord who heals, must have been for the Israelites (and for us). God's people were dying of thirst with only bitter, poisonous water on hand. God took their physical need and turned it into a spiritual issue. Out of a bitter experience God revealed Himself in yet another sweet, comforting way, as "Jehovah heals."

The Cast-Down Sheep

In the Old Testament, "to heal" is often used of a physician and means *to restore* or *to cure.* And just who does *Jehovah-Rophe,* the Great Physician, heal? He heals and restores those of His who are cast down.

There's a beautiful picture for us here. You see, shepherds throughout time have applied the term "cast down" to any sheep that's turned over on its back and can't get up by itself. A heavy, fat, or long-fleeced sheep will lie down comfortably in a little hollow in the ground. Next it rolls over on its side to stretch out and relax in the green grasses. But being in a hollow, the sheep's center of gravity may suddenly shift, pitching it onto its back so that its feet no longer touch the ground. Despite the poor sheep's struggling efforts, it can't get upright.

This is a sheep that is "cast down." And, interestingly, it's usually the largest and strongest sheep that are the most easily cast down. If it's cool or cloudy or rainy, a cast-down sheep can survive in this position for a day or two. But if the weather is hot and sunny, a cast-down sheep will be in critical condition in a few hours. If the shepherd doesn't arrive on the scene soon, the sheep will die.

The Course of Restoration

As I read about the process of restoration described by a shepherd in New Zealand, there were three stages involved.

> *Stage 1—Finding the cast-down sheep.* The caring, compassionate shepherd knows each and every one of his sheep. And he also knows when one of his flock is missing, so he sets out to find his wayward sheep, searching and surveying the range for the obvious form of a sheep.

> *Stage 2—Restoring the cast-down sheep.* Restoration can be quite involved, depending on the condition of the cast-down sheep. If, for instance, the sheep has been in its helpless condition for only a short time, all it takes from the shepherd is a gentle roll of the sheep over onto its feet, and, with only a few stumbles and wobbles, that fortunate sheep is back on its way to the fold.

> However, if the sheep has been down for some time, restoring it takes a great deal of patience, time, and care. First the sheep is gently rolled over. Then its legs are rubbed and massaged by the shepherd to revive circulation. Next comes the sheep's head, which is propped up on the shepherd's knee and stroked and caressed and held for a time by its loving caregiver.

Following this tender attention, the sheep is physically lifted onto its feet by the shepherd. As the weak and wobbly sheep leans against the strong legs of its shepherd, it takes its first few steps, fully supported by its master. It may take a full hour to get the sheep walking again. Finally it staggers away on its own, circling near the shepherd, who may have to rush over and pick it up again…and again…and again until it's completely steady.

Stage 3—Following the cast-down sheep. But the shepherd isn't done yet. Not until the sheep that was cast down takes its first bites of green grass does the shepherd know that all is well. And so the good shepherd follows and checks up on his recovering sheep until it is fully restored.[1]

⟶ Building Your Confidence in Him ⟵

And now it's time to shift from sheep to the soul. Life is hard! We're both familiar with its hurts and pains and inconveniences. You and I have tasted life's trials and sorrows. Unfortunately, many women are broken in spirit and crushed in heart and soul. Indeed, the prospects of becoming cast down are high as each new dawn and every new corner looms, fully loaded with trouble.

I'm just stating the facts of life—coping is a lifelong challenge. The good news is that we have a Shepherd—the Good Shepherd—to walk with us along life's way! We have…

> ⟋ *Jehovah-Rohi* who promises to care for us.
>
> ⟋ *Jehovah-Jireh* who promises to provide for us.

⇜ *Jehovah-Shalom* who promises to give us peace.

⇜ *Jehovah-Rophe* who promises to restore us.

So as New Zealand shepherd W.G. Bowen points out, "Problems are not the problem, but the problem is in trying to cope with problems on our own and with our own resources and in our own strength, or weakness, without the help of the Shepherd."[2]

Armed with the promise of healing restoration and confident in the presence of the Shepherd, you can walk through life with hope and certainty. With the help of the Lord, you can handle life's challenges and heartaches, even the valley of the shadow of death. What comfort your fainting heart has, knowing that in those stumbling times of discouragement and despair, of depletion and seeming defeat, the Shepherd will find you...restore and "fix" you...and follow you... until you are well on your way again!

⸻⸺

The Case of Elijah

Are you wondering what causes us to need God's healing touch? What takes us down or tempts us to give up? One such demise is caused by *not enough of the right things* (or *too much of the wrong things*). If we've been...

⇜ running too long—the Shepherd revives us.

⇜ running on empty—the Shepherd refreshes us.

⇜ running with the wrong people—the Shepherd replaces them.

- running away—the Shepherd retrieves us.
- running scared—the Shepherd refocuses our attention.

Do you remember that it's generally the largest and strongest sheep that become cast down? That certainly is true in one particular instance noted in the Bible. Elijah, the most famous and dramatic of Israel's prophets, a man who performed many miracles for God (and one of God's largest and strongest sheep!), succumbed to the problem of not enough of the right things.

Elijah was God's representative in a showdown with the priests of Baal and Asherah (1 Kings 18). After calling down fire from heaven and overseeing the slaughter of 450 of the pagan prophets of Baal, something happened. Elijah received word that Ahab's wife, Jezebel, was seeking to kill him (1 Kings 19).

This great man of faith ran. One woman was after him, and he took off, running and running and running.

He ran away into the wilderness.

He ran too long.

He ran too hard.

He ran scared.

He ran so far and so long and so hard that soon he was running on empty.

Falling down in weariness (much like a cast-down sheep!), Elijah rolled over and stuck his worn-out feet into the air. He gave up. He even asked God to let him die—indeed, to even kill him! And then the largest and strongest of God's prophets passed out in exhausted sleep.

What did God do? He brought healing care to His servant Elijah and restored him to usefulness:

- He gave him physical care—rest, food, and drink.

ᵛᵉᵛ He talked with him and listened to his discouragement, to his dismay, to his feelings of futility.

ᵛᵉᵛ He gave him something to do.

ᵛᵉᵛ He gave him a plan and some facts (1 Kings 19:4-18).

God kept right on restoring His precious prophet, never letting go and never giving up on him, working and loving until Elijah was fully recovered.

~Building Your Confidence in Him~

Oh dear! If the largest and the strongest sheep succumb to exhaustion, discouragement, and depression, is there any hope for little ewes like me...and you?

Before you give up, look at the causes *and* the cures for Elijah. They're going to be the same for you. God gave Elijah something to do. Why? Because Elijah had gotten *too comfortable*. He perhaps even liked moping around, sleeping, lying on the ground in a heap. And he'd gotten *too fat*. He certainly hadn't done much in more than 40 days. And he'd gotten *too independent*—he'd left his servant and assistant and companion behind and gone on alone. Elijah needed something to do...and that was a part of God's cure.

Do you fit "the Elijah profile"? Are you depressed or dismayed? Defeated or discouraged? Are you alone? Are you tired of life? Check out your situation:

ᵛᵉᵛ Have you gotten *too comfortable?* Are you lying around too much? Nibbling and nodding a little too often? Sprawled out in the green grass a little longer than necessary? Then do something!

⟹ Have you gotten *too fat?* When was the last time you really stretched yourself in some worthy effort? Really dug in and gave something your all? Really paid a price for something meaningful? Then do something!

⟹ Have you gotten *too independent?* The Bible tells us that being with others in the church body stimulates us, inciting us to good deeds and noble actions (Hebrews 10:24). God's people bring joy into our lives, keep us company, keep us on the right track, and keep us out of trouble! So do something!

Something to do is one of God's cures for the cast down—so take the cure and do something!

⟿

⟿ More Building Your Confidence Insights ⟿

The Lord heals. It's so like our Lord to pursue us, to continue after us when we run, to supply all our needs when we choose not enough of the right things and too much of the wrong things. What is the prescription for us that will help us confidently stand upright instead of becoming cast down? Try these two surefire remedies for health and healing.

Feed on God's Word. The Shepherd restores our

soul—not TV, not entertainment, not a sitcom, not food, not a drink, not a drug, not a vacation, and not another trip to the mall. And one way to touch the Shepherd and to experience His healing touch is to read and know His Word. "The law of the LORD is perfect, restoring the soul" (Psalm 19:7 NASB), and we can have direct contact with the Lord by feeding on His Word.

Commune with the Shepherd in prayer. Read another lesson on "shepherdology" from our friend from New Zealand:

> It is interesting to note that [in a flock] each sheep has a time of quietness and aloneness with his shepherd every day. Early in the morning the sheep would form a grazing line and keep the same position throughout the day. At some time along the way each sheep left the grazing line and went to the shepherd. The shepherd received the sheep with outstretched arms speaking kindly to it. The sheep would rub against the shepherd's leg, or if the shepherd were seated, rub its cheek against his face. Meanwhile the shepherd would gently pat the sheep, rubbing its nose and ears and scratching its chin. After a brief period of this intimate fellowship together, the sheep returned to its place in the grazing line.[3]

What a blessing to be able to leave the cares of life for a brief period and spend time in the outstretched arms of your Shepherd, rubbing, as it were, your cheek against His face in intimate fellowship through prayer.

⚊⚊

Do you have your answer to the question posed at the beginning of this chapter? About *how* we can go on when life has knocked us down? We can always go on because of the Shepherd and His healing touch. He comes after us in our pain and our utter despair, when we are down—so far down that we can no longer get up.

- ⚊ He touches us.
- ⚊ He heals our spirit.
- ⚊ He restores us when we're cast down.
- ⚊ He retrieves and fetches us home when we wander.
- ⚊ He draws us back when we're unsure.
- ⚊ He relieves us when we're hurt.
- ⚊ He rescues us when we're in danger.
- ⚊ And He finds us when we're lost.

Oh, give praise to and for the Shepherd now, for He restores your soul! The Good Shepherd finds and heals His sheep! Or, as verse three is also translated, "He found me when I was cast down and gave life to me again."[4] That's what our wonderful Shepherd does for you and me. No matter what happens in life, no matter how or how often you become cast down, God heals you. He restores you. He gives you life and strength to go on *with* Him.

*Your wonderful Shepherd not only takes care
of your physical requirements:
He also sees to your spiritual needs.
He ministers to the spirit and soul
as well as the physical body.*

6

God Will Guide You

He leads me in the paths of righteousness
for His name's sake.

PSALM 23:3

I will instruct you and teach you
in the way you should go;
I will guide you with My eye.

PSALM 32:8

*I*t takes 21 days to eliminate a bad habit and replace it with a new one." Are you familiar with this general law of behavior change? Better yet, have you tried it? I have...numerous times—and with numerous habits. From seeking to develop the habit of prayer to stopping in-between-meal snacking, from procrastination to better using my time—I've tried this "21-day miracle cure." But I've found that it takes much longer to break old habits and create new ones. The "old" or "bad" or "less efficient" ways are so deeply ingrained that it can seem impossible to improve or change them.

Why? Because of *repetition*. A habit is a custom or practice acquired by repetition. A habit is an action that, due to *repetition,* increases in performance and decreases in resistance. By repetition an action becomes automatic.

How do our habits work with the restoring and healing the Lord offers? Psalm 23, verse 3, reveals yet another role the Shepherd takes in our lives: "He leads [us] in the paths of righteousness for His name's sake." If we stay close beside Him and walk where He guides us, our habits will honor His name, and we'll harvest the fruits of righteousness. We'll develop holy habits!

So let's step on the Shepherd's path and learn what it means to have His reassuring promise to guide us and help us walk in His ways.

The "Paths"

A very simple way to understand the "paths of righteousness" the Good Shepherd leads us on is using the word "tracks." In bygone days tracks were made by the frequent passage of wagons. The more often a path was taken, the deeper the wheels cut into the soil, until the tracks became plain and obvious. Eventually deep ruts developed.

When I was in Israel studying and preparing for my book *Beautiful in God's Eyes: The Treasures of the Proverbs 31 Woman,* I saw the same thing happen regarding the paths sheep take on the hillsides. Because sheep habitually take the same way each time they go out to graze, their paths cut deep patterns into the sides of the slopes. In fact, many of the mountains look terraced because of the sheep paths creating stair-step ledges.

Later, as I was writing on the life of the Proverbs 31 woman, I discovered in verse 27 the use of "paths" or "ways" or "tracks": "She watches over the *ways* of her household." These words picture a woman acting as a shepherdess to her household. She carefully notices the patterns of her home life. These are the *ways* of her household, the general comings and goings, the habits and activities of the people at home. The Hebrew word for *ways* means tracks made by constant use. They're like the footpath that cuts across a lawn due to repeated use.

Well, the beautiful overseer-of-the-home from Proverbs 31 observes all that goes on in her home. Our watchwoman is aware of all the habits and any changes in habits. Nothing catches her by surprise. She keeps up-to-the-minute on the status of her family members and the general flow of her home. She's aware of everything that goes on within its walls.[1]

ᵔ *Building Your Confidence in Him* ᵔ

Let's stop a moment and consider your heart and home. If you have a family, think about how deeply you love and care for that family. About how concerned you are about the pattern of each precious life under your roof. Every mother and homemaker knows the pain of watching one of her flock struggle, stumble, and stray. We hurt as those we love make choices that lead them down unhealthy paths. We dread the sure and awful outcomes that await our loved ones if they continue down such dreadful paths.

Yes, we hurt, but we also act! With hearts wrung with agony, we roll up our mothering sleeves and do all we can to correct the situation. We create new rules and set narrower boundaries. We institute new disciplinary methods that carry more severe consequences. Why? All because of love—parental love.

Now can you begin to grasp the Shepherd's great divine love for His sheep? Just as you notice the *ways* of your household, so God notices the *ways* of your paths. Just as you hurt and agonize over those you love, so He cares for you. And just as you move to correct and guide your flock back onto a more profit-able path, so God leads and guides you in "the paths of righteousness."

※

The "Paths of Righteousness"

So far we know that our Shepherd is leading us. And He's leading us in "paths." And now we discover that those are "paths of righteousness." That means they're stiff or straight paths. For instance, in the Bible *righteousness* is used in these ways:

- ❧ *With men,* righteousness indicated a full measure. Measurements and weights were to be just and right.

- ❧ *With God,* righteousness indicated a full measure in the spiritual sense—offering to Him what was sincere versus half-hearted and shoddy.

- ❧ *With a court,* righteousness indicated a full measure of righteous judgment. Judges and offi-cers were to render justice and make things right.

Stiff and straight. This doesn't sound very pretty or seem too desirable in our loose times, does it? But, dear one, we have a God who is zealously interested in righteousness, and we have a God who promises to guide us into righteous paths.

～Building Your Confidence in Him ～

It's true that we live in an age that honors looseness. Praise abounds for those who can "flex and flow," who can roll with the tide, who can give and take, who are skilled at compromise and in finding middle ground.

But we're the righteous saints of a righteous God! And He makes sure we walk rightly, following Him in integrity. And He is faithful to tell us in His Word exactly what those paths are. He clearly spells out what He considers right and wrong...what He's determined is in and out...what He brands as good and evil. Gracious in other areas, God is stiff and straight about *His* way. In fact, He labels *His* way as *the* way and commands that we walk in it—"This is *the* way, walk in it" (Isaiah 30:21). As the Shepherd whose responsibility is to lead us, He plainly defines "the paths of righteousness" and guides us there.

～✻～

The God of Righteousness

Considering God's righteousness, let's look at yet another descriptive name of our wonderful Lord: *Jehovah-Tsidkenu* (pronounced sid–káy-noo). This name means "Jehovah our righteousness" and first appears in Jeremiah 23:5-6. Here are a few brief facts about the scene.

- ✻ The kingdom of Judah was falling apart.

- ✻ Judah was sinning grievously, even polluting the house of the Lord.

- ✻ God sent His prophets to warn His erring people, but their messages went unheeded.

- ✻ God sent His prophet Jeremiah to predict that Judah would be taken captive.

That was the bad news.

But because of God's promise to King David to establish his kingdom forever (2 Samuel 7:16), Jeremiah also prophesied some good news—Israel would be restored to the land, and Jehovah would raise up to David a Righteous Branch—*Jehovah Tsidkenu* (Jeremiah 23:5-6).

God was dealing with His sinning people, and they would be chastised. But in the end He would restore them, and He would produce a Righteous Branch (*Jehovah-Tsidkenu*). That Righteous Branch of David we now know as the Messiah, Jesus Christ.

⤳ *Building Your Confidence in Him* ⤳

Let's pause and consider this example (albeit a negative one!) of God's people in Jeremiah's time. They strayed from God's ways, sinned grievously, and failed to pay attention to God's pleas and instructions. Therefore, they were chastised.

And so, as women who love the Lord, we must bluntly ask ourselves if there are any areas in our lives where we know we're off track, out of God's will, wandering off His path of righteousness. Are there any choices of disobedience we're repeatedly making so they are becoming unholy habits?

Here are seven time-proven "A" practices that will help us leave the ruts of bad habits and the paths of sin and rush to the side (and safety!) of God's guidance:

⤳ *Admit your sin* and acknowledge it as disobedience.

⤳ *Ask for accountability* from other trusted Christians.

⪼ *Arm yourself adequately* with prayer and with Scripture.

⪼ *Associate with other Christians* who possess the habits you desire.

⪼ *Abolish all stumbling stones* from your environment.

⪼ *Aim at walking beside the Shepherd* one day at a time.

⪼ *Acquaint yourself more intimately with Jesus* and His righteousness.

How blessed you are to have a God who cares for you, who promises to lead you and guide you out of your own unprofitable ruts and into His paths of righteousness!

﹌

The Purpose of God's Guidance

Besides His great love for us, there's a greater reason God guides us. It's found in the last part of Psalm 23, verse 3: "He leads [us] in the paths of righteousness *for His name's sake.*" To bring glory to Him. In ancient Hebrew thought, a name was normally connected to the character and personality of the bearer, and this beautiful phrase—"for His name's sake"—means maintaining one's reputation. God's name points not only to a descriptive title for Him, but also to His very nature.

For *His* sake He leads us to do what is right. Why? Because if *we,* His sheep, sin and stray, we tarnish *His* reputation. So for the sake of His own name, as well as for our good, He points us in the right direction.[2] His name is *Shepherd* (Psalm 23:1), and He is the Good Shepherd—the Best Shepherd! Because of who He is, He must love and take care of us. His name demands it!

⤳ Building Your Confidence in Him ⤳

I remember all too well when Jim and I were up to our elbows in the business of child-raising. Peer pressure on our two girls was creating serious challenges for our family. It was at that time that Jim, as the shepherd of our household, began reminding our daughters that they were part of "the George household" and that in "the George household" our standards were such-and-such. Many times he told our girls, "We don't do that in the George household," or "That behavior's okay for others...but not for the Georges."

Far from being legalistic or demanding, Jim was setting a standard for our family and leading us as a family under the banner of that standard...for our sakes...but also for his sake. *Jim's* reputation as head-of-household was on the line. *Jim's* character was on trial through the conduct of his family (1 Timothy 3:4). As our head-of-household, Jim was responsible and accountable to God for loving and leading us in the right direction—in God's direction.

And we all benefited from having high standards set for us by a loving and concerned leader. Many "wrong" decisions and "wrong" choices were diverted because of Jim's loving leadership. And it's not that less-than-perfect decisions weren't made, or that "Shepherd Jim" didn't have to go out into a few highways and byways and fetch his sheep in from time to time (because, after all, sheep do have minds of their own). But the general pattern in our household was loving leadership and faithful following.

Can you relate this simple, daily, familiar illustration of family life to your own faithful following of the Shepherd? He is faithfully guiding and lovingly leading you. He has set forth His standards—His path—in His Word for you. And His name and reputation are at stake.

Is your following bringing glory to His name? He is leading you in the paths of righteousness for your sake *and* for His name's sake. Are you following in those paths for Him?

~~☙~~

⁓More Building Your Confidence Insights⁓

And exactly how does God guide you and me in the paths of His righteousness? These two practices have never failed to show me God's path:

#1—*Bible reading*. As someone has well warned, "Make sure the path you choose leads you at last to a place where you want to be. A careful traveler will study the road map before setting out!" Beloved, our road map for the right path is the Bible. Between the covers of our Bible we have the mind—and the map—of God! Indeed, His Word is a lamp unto our feet, ever lighting the path of righteousness…one step and one decision at a time (Psalm 119:105).

#2—Prayer. When we were missionaries in Singapore, I learned from an artist who attended my Bible study that in traditional Chinese painting, there is one outstanding object, usually a flower. That one flower on the canvas of our lives, dear one, is the will of God. God promises to guide us into His paths when we sincerely seek His will. When we chart out our map with earnest prayer, we'll end up on His path—the right path!

⤳⤳⤳

God is fulfilling His promise to guide you. Enjoying the blessings that come with His promise depends on how closely you follow Him. As a final heart-check, pray over these questions:

- ⤳ What are the desires of my heart?

- ⤳ Is my first desire to be in God's will—no matter what it is and no matter what it costs?

- ⤳ Am I living my life in a way that honors the Lord, that exhibits to the watching world what and where the paths of righteousness are?

- ⤳ Am I walking near the Shepherd—as close as I can—delighting in His guidance and allowing nothing to distract me from His paths?

- ⤳ Am I willing to go where He guides me...in the paths of righteousness...for His name's sake?

Just as you notice the ways of your household,
so God notices the ways of your paths.
Just as you hurt and agonize over those you love,
so He cares for you.
And just as you move to guide your flock
back onto a more profitable path,
so God guides you
"in the paths of righteousness."

7

God Never Leaves You

Yea, though I walk through the valley
of the shadow of death,
I will fear no evil; for You are with me.

PSALM 23:4

Lo, I am with you always, even to the end of the age.

MATTHEW 28:20

The area where we lived in Southern California was considered desert, but, believe it or not, we received enough rainfall each year to keep plants alive and growing. I do remember one seven-year stretch when our area was assessed as being in emergency drought status. Water use was greatly restricted. Public ads on TV educated us on conservation. No longer could we hose off our driveways and patios. Nor could we wash our cars using city water. Our lawns could only be watered on certain days at specific hours, and for an assigned number of minutes.

In the beginning of those drought years, one of my friends moved to a new home in nearby mountains. Observing the fire codes, she planted vegetation to keep her hillside from eroding and installed the prescribed automatic watering system to keep her foliage alive and protect her home against fire. Each time I visited her, I could see growth in her landscaping. On one visit I remarked about the suddenly glorious hillside vegetation with its flaming flowers and lushness of maturity. I've never forgotten my friend's comment: "It's because of the rain. All sunshine produces a desert...but rain brings forth flowers."

Yes, that was it! I hadn't thought about it, but the drought was over! (In fact, we were inundated with rain, bringing problems with mud slides and flash floods.) We'd been through seven years of sunshine, but the *rain* brought abundant growth. The *storms* had incited the plants to swell and surge and thrive. The darkness of clouds had brought about brilliance.

And, dear reader, so it is with life. As we walk through life beside our faithful Shepherd, the path of righteousness stretches through the sunshiny green pastures and beside glistening still waters...but it also winds down through the dark valley of the shadow of death.

The Way of the Path

As we continue our walk through Psalm 23, suddenly the path turns downward in verse 4. It begins to wind around difficult terrain. There's a precipice, perhaps. Or a steep riverbank. The water in the valley of shadows and darkness foams and roars, surrounded by jagged rocks. Passing through a deep and narrow gorge, we must press ourselves hard against battlements of rock and sheer walls of stone.

The imagery describes the valleys—or *wadis*—so familiar to the Holy Land, which is the setting of Psalm 23. It's wilderness. I've seen it and walked it myself. It's desert with pits, ravines, and caves, the dryness of drought, and the shadow of death. It's truly a no-man's land, a geography that signals danger and death.

Reading through the Old Testament reveals 18 uses of "shadow of death." This phrase refers to darkness...deep darkness...*very* deep darkness...thick darkness...and a darkness as dark as death. Its meaning includes the "death shadow" and the extreme dangers of the desert where death is dominant because of the harsh conditions.

~ *Building Your Confidence in Him* ~

Have you ever traveled down, down, down into dark valleys? Can you remember a time of foreboding or panic? Of suffering and sorrow? Of terror as darkness overshadowed you and swallowed you up as you journeyed into the unknown? I can pinpoint a few dark times in my life, including:

- ﹋ five years of wanting children and not being able to have any
- ﹋ ten days vigil beside my father-in-law's deathbed
- ﹋ three days beside my mother-in-law's deathbed (without Jim)
- ﹋ one year of watching my father decline and die
- ﹋ suffering through my mother's declining mind and eventual death
- ﹋ beginning months on the mission field as a stranger in a strange land
- ﹋ "mothering" times when things didn't go in the right direction.
- ﹋ a cancer scare

Yes, I've known darkness. I've tasted fear. But, friend, I can now praise God for those dark times. Why? Because I now know more about His promises.

He was with me through those times! Because I now know more about His grace. It was sufficient for me in those terrifying times! His gracious presence enabled me to journey *through* those valleys of darkness and death. As David, the psalmist, wrote, "Yea, though I walk *through* the valley of the shadow of death."

Perhaps even now you face the path of darkness or are in the valley of the shadow of death. The day that I taught this powerful verse at our women's Bible study, I jotted down four of the prayer requests for the day: One woman was facing a battery of physical examinations for an unknown malady, another had just lost a 10-year-old child through death, one of our missionaries was suffering physically on the field and lacked medical care, and another dear lady had a setback in her cancer treatment. And this represented *one* day and *one* group of women. Oh, how many more there are who walk in darkness and need to know the loving presence of our Lord!

It's true that the perilous valley is part of our path of life. Yes, life includes the shadows and dangers of chronic illness and pain, of loss of finances and security, of aging and disability, of medical tests and treatments, of surgeries and uncertain complications, of suffering loss and helping others who are suffering.

But we have reason to have hope and give praise! We can grasp the hand of God as we descend into the valley, into the devouring darkness. We can rest in the knowledge that He has trod this path too and knows what we're going through. And we can walk calmly— and confidently!—with Him, remembering He is with us always.

So *walk*, dear suffering one. Never fail to keep walking! Don't pause. Don't falter. Don't ponder. Just proceed. Move foreward! Know that as the Shepherd's dear sheep and as God's beloved child, the Lord is beside you to help you make it *through* the difficult time. You'll be comforted as you remember and lean on the promise that the Good Shepherd does not take His sheep into the valley of darkness to stay—but only to pass *through* it. "Yea, though I walk *through* the valley of the shadow of death..."

Walk in the Path

Wow! All seems dark, doesn't it? Everything seems hopeless in the valley. But David didn't end verse 4 or his psalm *in* the valley of the shadow of death. Nor will we stop and tarry in its foreboding darkness. Psalm 23 isn't meant to discourage us. Quite the opposite! *Every* shadow is produced by light. It's impossible to have a shadow without a light. Has that ever occurred to you?

And, our Lord *is* our light! He is the light of this world (Psalm 36:9 and John 1:4-9). He promises to be with us every step of the way. Indeed, *He* lights our path...one step at a time...one turn at a time.

That's how it was for the shepherds of old, and perhaps that's the image David is presenting in Psalm 23. Shepherds used to carry lamps made out of parchment folded much like a Chinese lantern. After lighting the little oil lamp inside the lantern, the shepherd would hold it up so it would give light to his feet—enough for one step at a time—as he led his sheep through the darkness.

⌁ Building Your Confidence in Him ⌁

As you and I walk through our valleys of darkness, it's so helpful and vital to remember these facts about God and our relationship with Him.

Remember...we walk by divine appointment. The valleys we enter are never accidental or the result of a mistake on God's part. No, we are *led* there by our all-wise, all-knowing, all-powerful Lord Jehovah. He knows the end from the beginning, the outcome of each and every pathway we tread. He orders our steps (Psalm 37:23). As the book of Proverbs notes:

- ⚬ A man's heart plans his way, but the LORD directs his steps (16:9).

- ⚬ A man's steps are of the LORD; how then can a man understand his own way? (20:24).

Remember...we walk in divine presence. No matter the twists and turns, the entanglements and obstacles along the path, David declares God is with us. We are never alone. God is always present and a constant source of strength and hope. He will never fail us.

When Jim's mother, Lois, lay dying, Jim was away in Germany on an Army assignment. Late one night during my vigil the nurses encouraged me to go home and get some rest. Only after securing their promise to call if there was any change in Lois' condition did I leave her side. Two hours later the ringing phone jarred me out of my sleep. It was the hospital telling me that Lois had died. As I rushed to the car (I'd slept in my clothes just in case), I wept—not with sorrow, but with anger. What happened? Why hadn't they called earlier? Why did Lois have to die alone?

But, oh, the precious assurance of Psalm 23:4 came to me: "Yea, though I walk through the valley of the shadow of death, I will fear no evil; for *You* are with me." Oh, blessed assurance! And what a blessed reminder! Lois hadn't been alone. She'd been with her Friend who was closer than a brother (or a son or a daughter-in-law or a nurse or a doctor). She had been—and *was!*—with her Savior, her Shepherd, all the way. Indeed, she had never been out of His presence!

Remember...we walk by divine grace. God promises that His grace *is* and *will be* sufficient for all our needs (2 Corinthians 12:9). Yes, we may experience fear when we imagine or anticipate future events, but the truth is that *when* we need God's marvelous grace, it will be here.

I love this story told by author Corrie ten Boom. As a child she once worried out loud, "Daddy, I don't think I could suffer or be a martyr for Jesus Christ. My faith is not strong enough."

Her father patiently answered, "Corrie, when you go by train from Haarlem to Amsterdam, when do I give you the train ticket? Several days before?"

"No, Daddy, the day I go to travel."

"And so it is with God. Now you do not need the grace to suffer, but if the moment comes when you need it, He will give you the grace. He will give you the train ticket right on time."[1]

I'm sure those words—and God's great grace!—strengthened Corrie when she suffered as a prisoner in a Nazi concentration camp and when her family died in the camps during World War II.

Remember...we walk by divine purpose. What is the purpose (or at least one of them) of the dark valleys we traverse? It brings us into greater intimacy with the Shepherd as we turn to Him for strength, guidance, comfort, and protection. Valleys are not meant to dishearten us or to provoke us or to trouble us. Valleys are merely passageways that bring us closer to our Lord. Just as we go out into the dark night to behold the brilliance of the stars, so God's presence shines the brightest in our valleys of deep darkness.

Walk slowly, dear pilgrim, when you go through darkness and death. As one person noted,

> It is a great art to learn to walk through the shadowy places. Do not hurry; there are lessons to be learned in the shadows that can never be learned in the light. You will discover something about God's ministries you never knew before. When we go into the valley of the shadow of death, we come so near Him that we look into His face and say not, "*He* is with me"— that is too formal, too far away—but "*You* are with me"![2]

Friend, walk with God *through* the dark valleys until you trust Him in the dark as much as you trust Him in the light.

⤳⤳⤳

The "I Will" of the Path

As we step back into Psalm 23, we encounter one of David's greatest "I wills" in the Bible: "I will fear no evil."

And remember, David had many opportunities to live in crippling fear. As a young teen he encountered lions and bears while watching over his father's flocks on the lonely and dangerous hillsides of Israel. He confronted the giant, Goliath, bearing only a sling and some stones. As a man, David was misunderstood, falsely accused, and hunted down by King Saul. He was forced out of his home and city and lived in the wilderness, hiding out in caves. As a warrior, David led and fought in many battles. He knew that fear is a great enemy. And David knew fear well!

But David also knew the Good Shepherd well. The boy and king learned to face the tragedies and terrors of life *with* the Shepherd and, therefore, *without* fear. He boldly declared, "I will fear no evil." Why? Because of the presence of God. David declared to God, *"You* are with me."

We too are not to fear. Just like David, we walk *with* our Lord, with our Shepherd. Whatever life brings, we will walk through it *with* our Shepherd, in His presence. Whatever losses we taste or stresses we bear, we will march through them *with* our Lord. Whatever enemies or threats to our lives we meet up with, we need not fear for He is *with* us. He is "a very present help in trouble. Therefore we will not fear" (Psalm 46:1-2).

And to assist us in achieving such fearlessness God tells us more than 80 times in the Bible to "Fear not!" Indeed, two frequent commands issued by Jesus were "Fear not" and "Do not be anxious."

✥ Building Your Confidence in Him ✥

Beloved, we are not to fear...period! We are not to be afraid of anything—any human, any situation, any calamity, any possibility, any uncertainty, any season, any loss. Fear on our part signals loudly a lack of faith in our Lord, who follows through on His promise to be with us every day, all the way.

And we are not to fear death either. Death is part of the valley of darkness. And we are not to be afraid as we walk through the valley of the shadow of death. Our dear Shepherd has promised to be with us—and He is and always will be!

Learn about the Shepherd from the writer who expounded on these words regarding death: "How can *that* be dark, in which God's child is to have the accomplishment of the longing desire of his life? How can it be dark to come in contact with the light of life?"[3]

Learn about the Shepherd from missionary Hudson Taylor's wife who uttered these words of encouragement to her grieving husband as she lay in her dying valley: "You know darling, that for ten years past there has not been a cloud between me and my Saviour...I .cannot be sorry to go to Him."[4]

Learn about the Shepherd from martyr John Stam who was beheaded with his wife in their valley of the shadow of death. He wrote to family and friends as their situation in China darkened: "If we should go on before, it is only the quicker to enjoy the bliss of the Saviour's presence, the sooner to be released from the fight against sin and Satan."[5]

Learn about the Shepherd from these words read at the funeral of my friend's dear mother-in-law:

Think…

> …of stepping on a shore and finding
> it heaven;
>
> …of breathing new air and finding it
> celestial air;
>
> …of feeling invigorated and finding it
> immortality;
>
> …of passing from storm and tempest
> to an unknown calm;
>
> …of waking and finding it heaven;
>
> …of taking hold of a hand and
> finding it the pierced hand of
> Jesus.[6]

And so, beloved, I encourage you to…

- *Sing* as you pass onward through the valley
  of the shadow of death, and let the notes
  of your joy vibrate against the walls of that
  valley.

- *Seek* greater knowledge of the Lord, your
  Shepherd, by faithfully acquainting yourself
  with His omnipotence and His omnipresence
  as revealed in His eternal Word.

- *Step* out in faith onto each and every path,
  knowing that the Lord is your Shepherd—
  not *was,* not *maybe,* not *will* be—the Lord
  is your Shepherd. He's with you on Sunday,
  on Monday, through every day of the week;
  in January, in December, and every month of

the year; at home, in China; in peace, and in war; in abundance and in poverty. *The Lord is your Shepherd.*[7]

Your Good Shepherd is ever-present with you!

*Just as you must go out into the dark night
to behold the brilliance of the stars,
so God's presence shines brightest in
your valleys of deep darkness.*

8

God's Comfort Is Only a Prayer Away

I will fear no evil; for You are with me;
Your rod and Your staff, they comfort me.

PSALM 23:4

Blessed be the God and Father of
our Lord Jesus Christ, the Father of mercies
and God of all comfort,
who comforts us in all our tribulation.

2 CORINTHIANS 1:3-4

Wasn't it splendid to spend a chapter beholding the wonderful presence of our wonderful Lord? How blessed we are to dwell in the light of the presence of our Shepherd who knows our every movement, thought, and word. He's acquainted with all our ways and loves us. Truly, such knowledge is too wonderful for us. It is high, and we can't comprehend it (see Psalm 139).

Let's linger a little longer. Let's take in a little more about what the presence of the Lord means to us. Let's give a little more thought to the comfort we enjoy in His company as we journey through the dark, threatening valley of shadows or the other paths God chooses to lead us on.

David wrote these promise-laden words in Psalm 23:4: "I will fear no evil; for You are with me; Your rod and Your staff, they comfort me." We know David was a shepherd and a warrior. And yet the warrior David is letting us know that he didn't find his comfort in the times of battle from the weakness of his enemy nor in his own strength. Instead he found comfort in the singular promise that the Lord, fully armed with His rod and His staff, was with him.

As David writes "for You are with me," he speaks of the omnipresence of the Lord. And this brings us to another name of God: *Jehovah-Shammah,* meaning "Jehovah is there."

Jehovah-Shammah

As with the other names and characteristics of God we've considered, there's a history behind *Jehovah-Shammah*. This assuring name of God comes out of the book of Ezekiel. Here are a few facts to help our understanding:

- ⅏ Ezekiel was one of God's prophets who was taken as a captive to Babylon with God's people (Ezekiel 1:1).

- ⅏ God asked Ezekiel to announce to the nation of Judah that they had been destroyed and removed from their homeland because of their sins (Ezekiel 2:5).

Talk about dark! Israel was at its lowest ebb in its history. And due to their chastisement, God's people had finally gone from being stiff-necked and hardhearted to being broken in spirit. It took being held as captives and slaves. Where they were once proud and obstinate, they at last came to the place where they lived in humiliation and genuine sorrow for their sins. In fact, their sorrow was so deep they could not even sing their beloved songs about the beauty of their homeland—of Zion, of Jerusalem. Instead they hung their harps on the willow trees...and wept (Psalm 137).

Shooting across the dark skies that hovered over this scene of sorrow and hardship came the dazzling promise of hope and consolation from God. Through Ezekiel God said He would *restore* the land of Judah and *return* His people to it. And Ezekiel announced that when they finally arrived home, Jehovah would also be there. In *Jehovah-Shammah* we have God's promise of restoration, comfort, and hope. "The LORD is there" (Ezekiel 48:35).

I know this name of God—*Jehovah-Shammah,* "the LORD is there"—sounds comforting and strengthening and evokes feelings of relief and reassurance. But there's more to it than mere emotion. The uniqueness and glory of Israel's religion had always been the presence of God dwelling in their midst. Whether by the Angel of the Lord or the Shekinah glory dwelling in the cloud and the pillar of fire and in the tabernacle and temple of God, God was present with His people. He dwelt in a city—the City of God (meaning literally *Jehovah-Shammah,* the Lord is there)—and He was the Helper of His people. Away from Zion, away from the City of God, there was turmoil, war, and ruin. But in Zion and with God there was safety, security, and tranquility. Why? Because the Lord was there—*Jehovah-Shammah!*

I'm sure you can see why the Israelites longed to return to their homeland. The hope of God's presence was there.

⌐ *Building Your Confidence in Him* ⌐

David realized the presence of God as he described "the valley of the shadow of death." And this is why you and I, as God's precious sheep, can confidently walk through any and every dark valley without fear. Why should we fear if we walk in the presence of God, our Shepherd? Why should we fear if the Lord is there? As Psalm 46:1-3 says,

> God is our refuge and strength, a very present help in trouble. Therefore we will not fear, though the earth be removed, and though the mountains be carried into the midst of the sea; though its waters roar and be troubled, though the mountains shake with its swelling.

This is one of my favorite biblical promises. I memorized it long ago because I loved its sentiment. I liked the feeling I experienced when I meditated on the fact that God is my very present help in times of trouble. And one day, January 17, 1994, to be exact, the earth under me moved and the mountains around me shook. That was the day of the devastating 6.8 Northridge, California, earthquake.

Northridge was three miles from my home...and 52 people died that day. A tremor is one thing, but a full-fledged earthquake is quite another. And having one occur at 4:31 AM in the darkness of night is even scarier. What made it even worse was that I was alone.

Now, picture me and a killer 6.8 earthquake in the wee hours of the morning. In the terror of that black night, I'm glad to report that verse 4 of Psalm 23 came to me! "Yea, though I walk through the valley of the shadow of death, I will fear no evil; for You are with me." I was there...*in* that valley—but so was my God and Shepherd!

As gigantic aftershocks rolled and roared through our area only minutes apart, causing still more devastation and terror, Psalm 46 also came to my rescue in a still small voice out of the recesses of my heart: "God is our refuge and strength, a very present help in trouble. Therefore we will not fear."

I learned then and there about the power of the promised presence and comfort of the Lord. About *Jehovah-Shammah*. About the Lord who is always present. He is there...in the stillness beside a quiet stream...and in the shaking of the mountains. At the hearth at home...and in the hospital. In accusations... and in acquittals. In trials...and in triumphs, in pain... and in pleasure, in seasons of activity...and in aging. In prisons...and in paradise. He is there when we pass through the waters...and through the rivers...and through the fire (Isaiah 43:2). *Jehovah-Shammah*—He is there!

Isn't this poem incredible!

> Lord of all being!
> Throned afar,
> Thy glory flames from sun and star;
> Center and Soul of every sphere,
> Yet to each loving heart how near![1]

With confidence, repeat with me: *You are with me, dear God! So near! Therefore I will not fear!*

⚓

Comfort Is There

"Yea, though I walk through the valley of the shadow of death." Although the valley of darkness is one of God's paths, the trip through the valley is not pleasant. Crags and stones, extremes of cold and heat, deserts and steep mountain trails constantly threaten. There are poisonous snakes and vicious animals lurking.

> ⁓ *Building Your Confidence in Him* ⁓
>
> As English clergyman F.B. Meyer wrote, "If we've been told that we're supposed to be on a bumpy track, then every jolt along the way simply confirms the fact that we're still on the right road!"[2]

Here's another reason to take comfort. God, our Shepherd, is armed! As His beloved sheep we need never fear, whether by day or by night. Why? Because two distinct implements are in the Shepherd's hand and they bring comfort to our hearts: His rod and staff. You and I have the promise of divine comfort symbolized in these tools as we walk life's pathway.

The Rod Is There

The rod of a shepherd hangs at the shepherd's side or is sheathed in a long narrow pouch attached to his cloak. Most generally it's made of oak and is about two feet long. After carefully choosing a straight young tree, the maker tears up the oak. The bulb at the beginning of the root, which is about the size of a man's fist, is trimmed to make the head of a club. Next a hole is bored through the rod so it can be tied to the shepherd's belt or hang from his wrist like a riding crop. Sometimes two-inch metal spikes are driven into the club head so that one blow can kill an attacking animal or deadly snake.

Sheep really have no defenses. God didn't make sheep with claws, or speed, or tusks, or quills, or shells, or fangs. All that the poor sheep has for defense is the shepherd and his rod. Armed with this instrument of protection, the shepherd leads his sheep through tall grass, swinging the club back and forth to prepare the way for his sheep. And with his tool of defense, the shepherd can beat off the enemies of the flock—eagles, snakes, wild animals, mountain lions, bears, wolves, coyotes, and even rustlers.

⚯ *Building Your Confidence in Him* ⚯

I have a confession: Sometimes I feel defenseless as a Christian woman, sort of like a sheep without claws, horns, speed, tusks, and so forth. While others may use their mouths and swing their "rights"—and even their fists!—God asks His women to put on a meek and quiet spirit. We're called to gentleness and submissiveness (1 Peter 3:4). God prizes graciousness and sweetness in us (Proverbs 11:16). But I draw much comfort in the very last part of verse 4 of Psalm 23. David writes of God, "Your rod and Your staff, they comfort me." I take comfort in the promise that *God* will take care of me. He will always come to my rescue when I need Him. He will also guide me with His wisdom. The Lord is always there, and He will knock down my enemies! Here are some more comforting and confidence-building promises:

- ⚯ *He* shall bring forth your righteousness as the light, and your justice as the noonday (Psalm 37:6).

- ⚯ I will cry out to God Most High; to God who performs all things *for* me (Psalm 57:2).

- ⚯ Through God we will do valiantly, for it is *He* who shall tread down our enemies (Psalm 60:12).

> ⚊ I will be with him in trouble; *I* will deliver
> him (Psalm 91:15).
>
> ⚊ If I say, "My foot slips," Your mercy, O LORD,
> *will* hold me up (Psalm 94:18).
>
> ⚊ The LORD will perfect that which concerns me
> (Psalm 138:8).
>
> ⚊⚊

The Staff Is There

Not only does God defend us—He also directs us. He not only
protects us—He also points out the way. How? His rod and staff!
We know what the shepherd's rod is. What exactly is a shepherd's
staff? It's a much longer piece of wood—probably around six feet
in length. It helps the shepherd climb up, around, and over rocks
to survey the stability of the land before leading sheep over it. With
his staff, a shepherd can check out crevices and caves for snakes
and scorpions that could harm his sheep. And his staff is also used
to prod loitering sheep and separate those that fight.

A shepherd's staff has a crook on one end, similar to a "U."
For centuries a staff with a crook has been used as an instrument
of guidance and restraint. It's come to symbolize the wise control
of a shepherd over his sheep. The crook can be slipped around a
sheep's neck to restrain it or guide it. The crook can keep a sheep
from falling. And this marvelous device is also wielded to rescue
sheep. If a sheep falls, the shepherd can twist the crook until it
hooks into the sheep's wool and pull the sheep up until it is once
again on sure footing.

The staff is most valuable to the shepherd as he cares for his flock.
He can use it to draw the flock together and keep the sheep from
wandering. He can use it to guide the little lambs to their moms. He

can count each sheep when night falls by gently tapping each one on its head or back with the staff as it enters the sheepfold. And the shepherd uses his staff to communicate with his sheep as they trek and amble along their many paths together. A gentle touch of the staff becomes a gesture of intimacy while walking, even though the shepherd towers over the sheep.

The staff is also used to coax the sheep to follow. A tap on a back leg brings a sheep into position, and a tap on the head of the lead sheep tells it to lie down so that the others will follow suit.

⁓ *Building Your Confidence in Him* ⁓

Let me share some fine words from one of God's sheep:

> Regrettably, we do not always follow our Lord. Sometimes our zeal tapers. The flame of our passion for Christ burns low. We grow cold in heart. Prayer becomes a burden rather than a pleasure. Zest for Bible reading dwindles while zeal to win lost souls to Christ disappears. [We] drift into spiritual slumps. But praise God, He understands! His love will not let us go. Though we find ourselves wandering from His side, suddenly we feel the staff of His love tugging at our hearts.[3]

The touch of your Shepherd's staff is indeed wonderful! Welcome it. Even yearn for it. It brings you comfort and is proof of His constant presence and everlasting love. In Him is comfort as He touches you and guides you and cares for you.

And now, dear friend, before we turn our thoughts to other powerful promises from Psalm 23, let's review our "Five Steps for Successfully Handling Sorrow":

⇒ Remember the place: *the valley of the shadow of death.*

⇒ Remember the proclamation: *I will fear no evil.*

⇒ Remember God's presence: *You are with me.*

⇒ Remember God's protection: *Your rod and Your staff.*

⇒ Remember the promise: *God's presence will comfort me.*

Take comfort! The Lord who is always present
is there...in the stillness beside a quiet stream...
and in the shaking of the mountains;
at the hearth at home...and in the hospital;
in accusation...and in acquittal;
in trial...and in triumph; in pain...and in pleasure;
in seasons of activity...and in aging;
in prison...and in paradise.
He is there when you pass through the waters...
and through the rivers...and through the fire!

9

God Is Your Friend...
and So Much More

You prepare a table before me...
You anoint my head with oil;
My cup runs over.

PSALM 23:5

There is a friend who sticks closer than a brother.

PROVERBS 18:24

In the midst of affliction my table is spread;
with blessings unmeasured my cup runneth o'er;
with perfume and oil thou anointest my head;
oh, what shall I ask of Thy providence more?

J. MONTGOMERY

ake a minute to imagine this scene: You're in a desert fleeing
for your life. You're hot and panting as you run for your life,
pursued and hunted by the forces of a fierce enemy. At last you see
a tent. Desperate, you run toward it, exhausting your final ounce
of energy. You touch the tent rope, dare to lift the flap, and enter.

Suddenly you realize you've been expected, you're "the guest of honor," and you're safe!

Now imagine David, who spent many days and nights pursued by his enemies, as the painter of this friendly picture. In Psalm 23, verse 5, he writes, "You prepare a table before me in the presence of my enemies; You anoint my head with oil; my cup runs over." We've already learned that on more than one occasion David's life was at risk. Here's a quick review:

- As a young shepherd, David fought lions and bears...and the fierce giant named Goliath.

- As a servant to King Saul, David experienced many murderous attempts on his life from the hands of the very man he served.

- As a warrior, David fought and slew his "ten thousands" (1 Samuel 18).

- After his wife Michal (Saul's daughter) helped him escape from King Saul's house, David spent the next several years running from Saul's rage.

- Seeking food, shelter, and a sword, David escaped to the priestly outpost of Nob. David then ran to the King of Gath to avoid death at the hands of the Philistines.

- As an "outlaw," David headquartered in a cave in the wilderness. There in that wild and mountainous region, David was hunted like the animals that lived there.

- When he was king of Israel, David was forced to flee for his life into the desert, pursued by his son.

It was this David—David the fugitive—who wrote of finding a gracious host, sumptuous provision, and a friend in the midst of running for his life.

⤳ *Building Your Confidence in Him* ⤳

Our experiences with flight and persecution may not be as literal or dreadful as David's were, but we do have our bouts with enemies. There are people who make our life difficult, who hound us, who block us, who slander us, who delight in our demise, who persecute us. There are those who let us have it, who take up an active cause against us, who harass, browbeat, pick, and nag. There are those whose mission seems to be creating tension for us, making sure we never relax.

When I think of trials, I never fail to think of Hannah, a woman noted in 1 Samuel, chapter 1. She experienced firsthand the promise and reality of God's friendship. Childless and relentlessly provoked by her husband's second wife, Hannah had nowhere to turn. Hannah certainly fell into the category of one who was mercilessly persecuted by an enemy, an adversary, a rival. This "other woman" chided and taunted her year after year, scoffing and laughing at her because Hannah hadn't borne any children.

When Hannah went up to the house of the Lord in Shiloh to worship one year, she poured out her problems and woes to Jehovah. She essentially lifted the tent flap, entered into the presence and provision of the Lord, and talked to her Friend who was closer than a brother (and in Hannah's case, her husband!). In God's presence, there was rest, there was camaraderie, there was help, and there was healing. Hannah left that place repaired, replenished, and rapturous!

You too have a friend in the Lord God. He will

provide solace for you from your enemies and your problems. You too can enter into the presence of the One who provides a haven of rest while you're on the run. Do you need to visit with Him now? Just lift the tent flap...just open your heart to Him who loves you unconditionally and completely...and delight yourself in His friendship!

⤳⎯⎯

The Server

Did you notice a change in language as we stepped into verse 5? Just as the scenery for a stage play changes between acts, there's a change in Psalm 23. A new image is introduced—the image of a host and guest. Suddenly we move from journeying *with* the Lord our Shepherd in the wilderness and fields as He leads us as a sheep to a scene of gracious hospitality and friendship *inside* His home. The setting shifts to show the psalmist as an honored guest enjoying the warm hospitality so characteristic of the Middle East, where Psalm 23 was written. The shepherd and sheep imagery is replaced by one of human intimacy, by feasting and friendship.

Furthermore, our psalm is progressing. Have you noticed the movement? In verse 4 we moved closer to God, becoming more intimate and realizing His divine protection through difficult times in the valley of darkness—even the harshness of death. We discovered that even in the valley we can find comfort and exclaim to our Good Shepherd, "You are with me!" We can experience the joy and security of Jehovah's protection and comfort.

But now, in verse 5, you and I are invited to focus on the promise of God's protection and the blessings of His friendship. David wrote: "You prepare a table before me in the presence of my enemies; You anoint my head with oil; my cup runs over." All along our journey we've needed God's protection, guidance, and provision. But here we're invited to experience the lavishness of His friendship as well.

The Supply

"You prepare a table before me." We've seen who our host and server is—the Lord Himself! But now we're allowed to see the supply our Host has heaped on His table for us. And it's truly a sight to behold! Oh, the labor, the work gone into spreading such a feast. The table is *prepared* for us. We're not unexpected guests, but anticipated ones. We're not drop-in guests, but invited ones. This isn't a quick snack where something—anything, even leftovers!—is thrown together. No! Preparations have been carefully made in advance. The table is elaborately furnished and liberally spread with food.

Truly this scene is a prototype of the ultimate, great table prepared by Christ for His bride at the end of the age (Revelation 19:9).

⤚ *Building Your Confidence in Him* ⤙

As a friend of God, my fellow traveler, you and I never have to worry about God's provision. As David declared previously, we shall not want. When God feeds a soul, then fed that soul shall be! God's table will never be bare. Indeed, God can furnish a table and give a banquet in the driest and harshest desert (Psalm 78:19)!

I read about a couple who announced to their families that they were no longer going to "do" Christmas, Thanksgiving, Easter, or birthdays, citing grocery shopping, cooking, and family dinners as a pain. Instead they were opting for sitting on the sofa with a stack of books and relaxing in front of the DVD with a dozen or so movies. The preparations and time for family gatherings were written off as a waste. (I was shocked and very sorry for the family!)

But our Lord prepares a table for you and me! He delights in producing a bounty beyond description! And He prepares what is best for us as we walk and wade through life. He prepares in advance, sets His banqueting table, and waits for us weary travelers to lift the tent flap and come in so He can minister to us. The thought of such lavish love can at times (depending on how tired or how wounded I am) move me to tears. This, precious one, is our God, the One who prepares a table in the wilderness for us when we can't go on, when we're completely worn out.

Are you following God's example? As a server in your home, are you supplying a table for those in your family and within your sphere of ministry? Are you pouring your love into gracious and generous preparations for your precious weary and worn-out family members and friends? Is your table set? Prepared? Furnished? Spread with the healthy nourishment needed to sustain their work and the battles they fight every day? We have the privilege of providing for those we love—just like our heavenly Father provides for us!

―⁂―

The Style

Before we look at the protection our Sovereign supplies to His guests, let's notice more about His wonderful provision for us. There are two additional marks of His hospitality and friendship and generosity toward His weary people that I want to point out.

First, the anointing. As David said, "You anoint my head with oil." (Oh the lavishness of our holy Host. He not only feeds us, but He anoints us too!) In yet another gracious gesture, our Lord anoints us with perfumed oil. This is a blatant act of luxury because oil is costly. It's also a symbol of festivity (The oil of joy replaces mourning—Isaiah 61:3). And it's a sign of happiness because ointment and perfume rejoice the heart (Proverbs 27:9). Chemists tell us of three unique pleasures and distinct qualities of oil:

- ✐ Touch—oil provides a smoothness.
- ✐ Sight—oil gives a brightness.
- ✐ Smell—oil supplies a fragrance.

All three elements combine to gratify our senses and are sources of delight. Imagine a running and hounded traveler treated to something so delightful and refreshing out of the bounty of a friendly, generous host.

Second, the filling of the cup. David adds, "My cup runs over." The magnitude of God's provision includes a well-filled cup. Used for drinking liquid at dinner or a banquet, cups were large and deep. The contents quenched thirst, refreshed the body, and invigorated the soul. Filled to overflowing—that's how God fills our cups! We'll be filled, saturated, completely satisfied.

⁓ *Building Your Confidence in Him* ⁓

There's no doubt about it. Our Lord's provision for us represents His thoughtfulness and generosity. As we tiredly and frantically enter into the refuge of

His tent in the desert, as we draw up the tent flap and behold the treasure of His table—a table prepared and filled and waiting—we see plenty of necessary food. But, dear one, there's also the oil of His joy and the filling of our cup to overflowing. We're truly stunned by God's abundance, not to mention His abundant goodness to us!

The sustenance, the oil, and the brimming cup do their job well and revive us. They simultaneously brace us, stimulate us, and delight us! They turn our time at God's table into a festival of joy.

When we think of all the riches of grace we have in our Lord God, we should burst forth with grateful and loving acknowledgment! As one person wrote,

> Nothing narrow, nothing stinted
> Ever issues from God's store;
> To His own He gives full measure,
> Running over evermore.[1]

~~~

A Sample of Blessings

How blessed we are to be called friend by the Sovereign God of the universe. Just think about it! Our divine Host is the awesome, all-powerful, all-knowing, always-present One. And yet He chooses us as His friends. Before we move on from this overwhelming (and humbling!) thought, let's pause and consider some of the many blessings you and I have in God's friendship. Spend just a few moments marveling at all that a visit with your friendly Host promises to be! These reflections are based on Psalm 23, verse 5.

~ *Ten Reflections on God's Promises* ~

➤ *Increased intimacy*—It's one thing to be a sheep with the Shepherd, but it's quite another to be a guest in His home. In our Father's house there is fullness of joy and pleasures forevermore (Psalm 16:11).

➤ *Divine care*—Jehovah prepares a table for us. Imagine how much He loves us to go to the effort to make everything perfect and lavish. Imagine the joy of feasting in God's presence, at His table, and on the fare from His hand. Truly, we shall never want.

➤ *Gracious amenities*—God anoints our heads with oil and fills our cup to overflowing. We can declare in joy and amazement, along with David, "Who am I, O LORD God...that You have brought me this far?" (2 Samuel 7:18).

➤ *A haven in a hostile world*—The psalmist speaks of enemies, but no enemy can come so near that God isn't even closer! No matter where we roam, no matter how many enemies pursue, no matter how hard the path, we need only lift the tent flap to His divine presence...and enjoy a retreat for our heart and soul. All who find their refuge in the Lord discover a true Friend, rest, refreshment, relaxation, renewal, and revival.

➤ *A shelter from the storms of life*—In our Father's house we can come in from the cold and experience the delicious heat of a

welcoming hearth. Come in from loneliness...
to fellowship. Come in from war...to peace.
Come in from darkness...to light. Come
in from danger...to safety. Come in from
famine...to feast. Come in from enmity...to
friendship.

⤳ *A warm welcome*—As we arrive, we find we
are expected. We've been anticipated. Preparations have been made in advance. Our Host
has been waiting to wrap His arms around
us in friendship. We're greeted with great joy
and love.

⤳ *A place to pause*—As we run from place to
place, event to event, we can always halt in
our Host's home. We stop. We breathe. We
pause. We enjoy. We sup. We rest. We fellowship. We regroup. In God's presence is
heaven on earth.

⤳ *A hospital*—As we arrive weary and worn,
haggard and breathless, battered and bruised,
bleeding and terrorized, our heads are
anointed and our wounds are bathed with the
oil of healing.

⤳ *A generous heart*—In the intimacy of His
house, our Host hovers over us, watching for
any and every opportunity to provide mag-
nanimously for us, continually refilling our
cups as we drink. He delights in pouring out
a generous portion.

⤳ *The blessings of friendship*—Our Host reflects
His true concern, His desire for our society

and fellowship, His loving sharing of all that comes from the heart of a true Friend—the lavishness of the oil of joy and the cup filled with blessings of every kind. God is our promised Friend.

It's absolutely true! As Psalm 23 promises, the Lord always meets the needs of His people!

> He spread'st a table in my sight,
> Thy boundless grace bestoweth;
> And O! What transport of delight
> From Thy pure chalice floweth![2]

*In your Father's house you can
come in from the cold…to the heat of a hearth.
Come in from loneliness…to fellowship.
Come in from war…to peace.
Come in from darkness…to light.
Come in from danger…to safety.
Come in from famine…to feast.
Come in from enmity…to friendship.*

10

God Will Always Protect You

[God is with me] in the presence of my enemies.

*O LORD my God, in You I put my trust; save me from
all those who persecute me; and deliver me.*

PSALM 7:1

*My times are in Your hand;
deliver me from the hand of my enemies;
and from those who persecute me.*

PSALM 31:15

I vividly remember one of those you-could-hear-a-pin-drop
moments. It was on a Sunday morning, and our congregation
was completely silent as our pastor told a story about a missionary
to cannibals. This dear man's wife had died on the ship carrying the
couple to their new mission station. When the boat finally docked, the
bereaved husband buried his wife on the shore of his new outpost
and camped out for several days and nights beside his wife's grave
to guard her body from the cannibals.

Later, when he began his ministry and contact was established with the islanders, the cannibals approached him with a question. They had watched the forlorn missionary stand vigil over his wife's grave, and they wanted to know, "Who were those men with you on the shore?" As the cannibals stalked the area, they'd kept their distance because the missionary was ringed by guards. The missionary had no idea what the islanders were talking about!

Who *were* those men? Perhaps in heaven we'll find out! My friend, the Bible is full of promises for God's protection. And it's packed with times God protected His people in the presence of their enemies. It's just as David wrote in Psalm 34, verse 7: "The angel of the LORD encamps all around those who fear Him, and delivers them" (Psalm 34:7).

One ordeal in the Bible reveals a hopeless situation for one of God's prophets. Elisha and his servant were surrounded by horses and chariots and a great host of enemy warriors. They came in the night and circled the city where they were. When Elisha's servant saw the armed masses, he cried, "Alas, my master! What shall we do?"

Elisha, ever the man of faith, calmly replied, "Do not fear; for those who are with us are more than those who are with them." And then Elisha prayed, "LORD, I pray, open his eyes that he may see."

And the Lord opened the eyes of the young servant. And what did he see? "Behold, the mountain was full of horses and chariots of fire all around Elisha" (2 Kings 6:17). God's protection was complete!

And it's true for us too. Out of His awesome power, God protects His people!

The Situation

For a minute, let's go back to Psalm 23, verse 5. We looked at the wonderful friendship we enjoy with God and marveled at His sumptuous provision of food, oil, and wine. Now we're going to look at more of verse 5 and note the unique situation in which God is providing His bounty: "In the presence of our enemies."

Remember, this psalm was written by David, whose life was filled with flight, fear, and reliance upon the hospitality of others. He experienced the enemies of the wilderness (beasts, scorching heat, and lack of water) and two-legged enemies—robbers, warriors, armies, and upstart rulers. Many times David found himself dining in the presence of his enemies.

The Scene

In our hurry-up lifestyle of meet-you-at-the-restaurant dinners and drive-thru eat-on-the-go lunches, it can be hard for us to envision the hospitality David sketches for us in verse 5, especially because it takes place in a desert and in a tent.

The abundant provision of the prepared and lavishly furnished table, the anointing of oil, and the cup running over reveals traditional Middle Eastern hospitality. In those days of traveling on foot and on beast, and in that land of desert, wilderness, and extreme heat and cold, travelers depended on the provision of strangers to keep them alive. It was a way of life.

⌒ *Building Your Confidence in Him* ⌒

I hope you'll take advantage of the many books available about offering Christian hospitality. And pray that you're developing a heart for inviting people to your home—those you know and love, those who live around you, those you don't know, and those who are needy. We must *choose* to nurture our hearts of hospitality. Sometimes we think hospitality will just happen, that it comes naturally, especially when we have the Good News of Christ to share. But the truth is that we must cultivate it.

Why not pick a time, invite some guests, plan a

menu, involve the family, prepare in advance (including prayer), and reach out to someone? Be faithful and follow through.

One day Jim announced that the missions board at our church (Jim is on that board) wanted each board member to invite our furloughing missionaries into our homes once a month. Jim and I sat down, calendars in hand, and picked the dates and the time. We talked through simple, doable menus, and planned the flow of the evenings—beginning and ending times, the serving of food, and a time of sharing and prayer.

As you develop a heart of hospitality and open your home to others, you're in for a double blessing. Your guests will be blessed...and so will you!

—☸—

Protection and Security

As we move ahead in Psalm 23, we arrive at protection and security. Eastern hospitality is synonymous with protection. To be someone's guest meant you were safe...at least for the duration of your stay inside the host's home.

Also, dining, especially in the presence of enemies, denotes a sense of security. Does that surprise you? In Middle Eastern culture, hosts are obligated to protect their guests at any cost.

One particular Bible story even shows this duty to protect one's guests vividly. When Abraham's nephew Lot had out-of-town guests, a mob came and asked him to surrender the visitors to them. But as host, Lot refused in the face of possible violence and reprisal.

Another instance illustrates the duty in reverse. It has to do with two brothers. One brother, Solomon, wasn't invited to a feast held by his brother Adonijah. Why? Adonijah planned to kill Solomon. And under the code of Eastern hospitality, Adonijah would be obligated to protect Solomon if he came to his house (1 Kings 1).

To be a guest included being protected.

Victory

Another Eastern custom is portrayed when David writes, "[dining] in the presence of my enemies." In David's day enemies who were conquered in battle were forced to watch the victory celebration. Sometimes a prisoner was chained to each pillar in the victor's palace to "feast" his eyes on the celebration.

⟶ *Building Your Confidence in Him* ⟵

Our enemies...sigh. I've been reading through the book of Psalms again. Once more I'm hit by how much of David's poetry centers on his bouts with enemies. He moans to God, "O Lord, I have so many enemies. How long will they ruin my reputation? They maul me like a lion. Lord, have mercy on me. See how I suffer at the hands of those who hate me" (see Psalms 3, 4, 7, and 9).

Enemies. They seem to be a fact of life on earth. But we're not to hate them. We aren't even to fight them. We aren't to fear them. We aren't to fret or worry about them. And we aren't to envy them. Instead, we are to do as David did—cry out to God. We are to pray *for* our enemies. We are to pray *about* them.

And we're also to *count on God's promises*. He promises to bring forth our righteousness as the light (Psalm 37:6-7). He promises to avenge us. And He promises to protect us. Our sovereign, all-powerful

God controls the universe—and that includes those who are our enemies. Compared to God, our enemies have no power. They can't frustrate God's good plan or His promised protection and victory.

Yes, you live in the midst of deadly enemies. And yes, they can make your life miserable. But remember, they won't have ultimate victory! You will safely feast in the presence of your enemies and in spite of your enemies! That's a promise from your all-powerful, loving God.

⟶⟵

Our Savior, Jehovah-Nissi

There's another reason why we need never worry about losing God's protection. He protects us as a Savior because He is *Jehovah-Nissi,* meaning "the LORD is my banner."

As we've seen with the other names of God, there's usually an exciting background. For *Jehovah-Nissi* look to the book of Exodus, chapter 17. God's people were wandering in the wilderness. When the Amalekites attacked them, Moses, their leader, went into action. Here's a quick summary:

First, Moses appointed Joshua to lead Israel into battle.

Second, Moses assured Joshua that he would stand on top of a hill with his staff—the rod of God—in his hand. While Moses' staff was lifted into the air, the battle went well. In the end, Joshua won the clash.

Third, Moses built an altar to celebrate Israel's victory and named the altar *Jehovah-Nissi,* meaning "The LORD is my Banner" (Exodus 17:15).

The name Moses chose, *Jehovah-Nissi,* revealed Israel's confidence that God was the One who gave them the victory. It was also a reminder that God was the One they should rally around as their banner in future skirmishes.

A "banner" in ancient times was a bare pole with a bright ornament on the top. This ornament, or ensign, glistened and shone in the sun. In fact, the Hebrew word for banner means "to glisten." At the time of the battle with the Amalekites, the banner was Moses' staff, sometimes referred to as the rod of God. Later, in another crisis, Moses lifted up a pole topped with a bronze serpent that saved the life of every Israelite who had been bitten by a poisonous snake (Numbers 21:9).

With incidents such as these, it's easy to understand how a "banner" or an emblem on a pole came to signify miracles. Ultimately, it was a sign of deliverance and salvation, a sign of God's protection.

God's rod in Moses' hand on that victorious battle day became a symbol and a pledge of God's presence and power to His people in the presence of their enemies. Moses experienced *Jehovah-Nissi*— "The Lord is My Banner"—in the presence of Israel's enemies.

David, when he wrote these lines in Psalm 23, anticipated ultimate victory and deliverance *in the presence of his enemies* because he rallied under God's banner of protection in His home as His guest.

↝ *Building Your Confidence in Him* ↝

You and I never have to worry about God's protection! I like this strong example of faith in *Jehovah-Nissi's* protection in the life of Martin Luther. When making his way into the presence of an enemy (a cardinal who had summoned him to answer for his heretical opinions), Luther was asked by one of the cardinal's servants, "Where shall you find shelter if your patrons and protectors should desert you?"

Luther answered, "Under the shield of heaven!"

Rejoice, my friend! *Always* rejoice because *Jehovah-Nissi* is your banner, your protector, your rescuer, your deliverer, your shield, and your Savior.

⇢

We've witnessed the situation—*the presence of enemies.* We've experienced the scene—*the safety and protection of our divine Host.* And we've beheld our Savior—*Jehovah-Nissi,* the Lord our Banner. Isn't it wonderful how we're fully cared for and fully armed with the protection of our God!

- ⇢ So as you face adversaries, remember the ultimate victory is yours because of God's great power…even in the presence of your enemies.

- ⇢ As you rally under His name *Jehovah-Nissi* and look to Him and the standard of His banner, remember you are protected…even in the presence of your enemies.

- ⇢ As you, in faith, lift up *Jehovah-Nissi* high in your heart, remember deliverance is yours…even in the presence of your enemies.

If God is on your side, what does it matter who is against you!

Here are a few more moving words from the hymn, "Like a River Glorious." They're so appropriate as we're challenged to totally trust in God's promise to protect us.

Hidden in the hollow of His blessed hand,
Never foe can follow, never traitor stand...
We may trust Him fully all for us to do.
They who trust Him wholly find Him wholly true.[1]

—————— ❈ ——————

*Your enemies have no power because
your sovereign, all-powerful God
controls the universe—
and that includes controlling those
who are your enemies.
They cannot frustrate God's good plan or
His promised protection and victory!*

—————— ❈ ——————

11

God Is Your Hope

Surely goodness and mercy shall follow me
all the days of my life.

PSALM 23:6

Through the LORD's mercies we are not consumed,
because His compassions fail not.
They are new every morning;
great is Your faithfulness.

LAMENTATIONS 3:22-23

All the streams of goodness and mercy flow freely
from God's fountain—God's pardoning, protecting, sustaining, and
supplying goodness and mercy...and
they follow us as surely as the water
out of the rock followed Israel.

MATTHEW HENRY

As we enter this final verse of the Twenty-third Psalm, we must turn a corner in our faith. Like a ship setting out to sea, we must leave the familiar shore and all that is seen... and sail on the winds of faith into the unseen. We turn our focus away from looking at what we know to be true of God's past and present care for us…and look to His promises to take care of us in the future. This will be quite a voyage—and a voyage of faith! A humbling and yet exciting discovery of our relationship with our Shepherd.

The Box

One day quite a few years ago, I really had my eyes opened as to just how dependent I am on others. Jim and I were moving things out of our home office to make way for some structural repairs needed because of earthquake damage. As I came to a small metal box, I stopped packing. Its label, scrawled with a black marker on a strip of masking tape, read "Finances." Wondering what this could be, I undid the latch and peered into the box.

What I found inside that small gray container was humbling… and encouraging: a bulging stack of receipts saved over the decades, proof of the payments Jim had faithfully made into his retirement and pension plans. There were also documents that verified his contributions to his medical and life insurance policies and to his social security account. Jim provides for my everyday needs. But because of what was inside this box, I was made aware, once again, of how his care for me extends into the future. I was humbled and encouraged by Jim's love and provision.

Goodness and Mercy

Now, my friend, whether we're married or single or young or old, verse 6 of Psalm 23 is like the box. It's a clear promise to you and me of God's provision for the future: "Surely goodness and mercy shall follow me all the days of my life." Individuals can scheme and dream of ways to care for us…but God *can* and *will* and *does* care for us—every day. He will get the job done! It's His promise!

Looking Back…and Up

I'm sure you've enjoyed many Fourth of July celebrations. You know the thrill of the brilliant bursts and loud booms and hissing sizzles of exploding fireworks. Looking back at the profusion of promises God makes to us in Psalm 23 is like looking at a show of fireworks!

- In verse 1—God promises us care and provision. *"The LORD is my shepherd; I shall not want."*

- In verse 2—God promises us wisdom and daily bread. *"He makes me to lie down in green pastures; He leads me beside the still waters."*

- In verse 3—God promises us guidance and restoration. *"He restores my soul; He leads me in the paths of righteousness for His name's sake."*

- In verse 4—God promises us companionship and comfort. *"Yea, though I walk through the valley of the shadow of death, I will fear no evil; for You are with me; Your rod and Your staff, they comfort me."*

- In verse 5—God promises us safety, joy, and fellowship. *"You prepare a table before me in the presence of my enemies; You anoint my head with oil; my cup runs over."*

Yes, God takes care of our every need each and every day of our lives! He has in the past, He does in the present, and He will in the future!

In Psalm 23, verse 6, David now adds a new element of hope with an upward look: "Surely goodness and mercy shall follow me all the days of my life; and I will dwell in the house of the LORD forever." Our walk with God, with our Good Shepherd, shifts from the present tense (*is, makes, leads, restores*) to future tense (*shall* and *will*). We're assured that God has planned and knows our futures, and He promises to take care of our every need forever!

∼ Building Your Confidence in Him ∼

A rusty tin box filled with cracked, faded, aging papers is one thing, but "the Book"—the living Word of God, the Holy Bible—is quite another! When it comes to promises for the future, the box of insurance and asset papers give a little comfort along life's path, but the promises made by God in "the Book" take us all the way through life…and beyond!

Did you know that estimations of the number of promises in the Bible range from 8,810 to 30,000?[1] While those to whom the promises were made are sometimes specific, there remains an immeasurable number of promises that are shot directly from God's heart to yours. Be sure you pore over what's in "The Book"! Familiarize yourself with each and every word of God's Word. Handle and touch and count each and every priceless promise of hope. Treat them as pearls, as gems, as precious jewels, each one of them making you wealthy. Keep them as treasures, but also wear them often. Memorize them and make them your own.

As one translator marvels,

> Through [God's] might and splendour
> He has given us His promises, great
> beyond all price" (2 Peter 1:4).[2]

And, as King Solomon discovered and passed on to us, "There has not failed one word of all His good promise" (1 Kings 8:56).

∼∿∼

Moving from Experience to Faith

"Surely." David begins verse 6 with a profound "surely" (and I like to think that in his mind David added a series of exclamation points after it). David is looking back at all that God had done for him and all He provided for him. He's highlighting how much God cared for his daily needs as they arose along the way.

And with the word "surely," David does an about-face. He turns 180 degrees, looks the future right in the face, and confidently declares, "Surely goodness and mercy shall follow me all the days of my life." With this statement, David is moving from life experience to faith. He knows he's under God's protection. His head is anointed with perfumed oil. His every need is being completely satisfied. With faith and confidence built out of the lessons of the past, David knows every moment of his future will be packed with God's richest blessings. *"Surely!"*

As the sweet hymn "Do Not Worry" asserts,

> Seek first, then, your Father's kingdom
> And His righteousness on high.
> All these things will then be given;
> God will not neglect your cry.
> So fret not about tomorrow;
> God directs the future, too.
> Though each day will bring its troubles,
> Trust in Him—He'll see you through.[3]

Well, dear friend, *hope* is what verse 6 is all about—hope for all our tomorrows. And for all our forever-days!

⸺ *Building Your Confidence in Him* ⸺

As we dare to peek down the dark corridor of times to come, are your heart and mind filled with hope or with fear? Our natural tendency is to fear the unknown. What we don't know and don't understand generally bothers us and shakes our confidence:

When we look...

- *at our possessions,* we wonder, *Will there be another earthquake, another hurricane, more flooding, devastating blizzards?*

- *at our families,* we wonder, *Will my children and grandchildren make wise decisions? Will they follow Christ? Will my other relatives come to know the Lord?*

- *at our finances,* we wonder, *Will I need to get a job? Will I get laid off? Is there really enough money for retirement? What if my husband loses his job or dies?*

- *at our health,* we wonder, *Will the next physical exam reveal cancer...in me or my husband or children? Will a disabling disease set in? Will there be years of suffering?*

- *at death,* we wonder, *What will cause it? What will it be like? How will my family cope, and what will happen to them?*

We can easily get caught up in wondering, *Is there really hope?* Friend, that's exactly when and where this precious promise of hope in verse 6 comes to our rescue! Not only can David confidently proclaim, "Surely goodness and mercy shall follow me all the days of my life," but as God's precious child, you can too!

If you're not quite sure, take an inventory. List how the Lord has faithfully and successfully shepherded you in and through the past. Based on that and on His promises given in His Word, will He faithfully and successfully shepherd you in and through the future? Of course!

As His cherished sheep, you never have to lack hope. You have His promised goodness and mercy to cling to and depend on and celebrate all the days of your life. God's promises should light a candle in your heart and create a blaze of glorious hope that dispels any of your doubts about the future. Realize you face the unknown with the known—with the proven, extended care of God, your Good Shepherd, who is the same yesterday, today, and forever.

Praise the Lord!

―※―

Seven Reasons for Hope in the Future

When Jim and I moved from Oklahoma to California, we took half a day out of our drive west to see the Grand Canyon. Oh, my! What a thrill! What a sight! You know how it usually goes in national parks. We arrived, stopped, looked, and took pictures. We drove along the canyon rim, halting at every viewing site of this vast canyon. Each time we parked the car, got out, and took a short hike to the little lookout stations. Out came the camera and Jim would take another photo of the canyon—from a different angle than the last shot. On and on we went, repeating this stop–hike–take photo routine.

And that's a great way to look at verse 6 in Psalm 23. We have seven shots, seven features, seven angles, seven different views of the same verse. We'll look at four of them here and three in the next chapter. You'll find plenty of reasons for confidence and hope for the future in these verses!

Are you ready for an even greater blessing than the abundant food, anointing of oil, and running-over cup we experienced at God's table in verse 5? Prepare for the goodness and mercy of the Lord!

1. God's Continued Goodness

Even though we've seen, tasted, and witnessed God's goodness for five verses in this psalm, what we see in our first view of verse 6 is God's *goodness* in our future: "Surely [God's] *goodness*...shall follow me all the days of my life." And what is God's goodness? It is the sum total of all His attributes. When Moses asked to see God's glory, God answered, "I will make all My *goodness* pass before you" (Exodus 33:19). As another of my favorite psalms simply says, "The LORD is good" (100:5).

God's goodness will follow and accompany us for the rest of our lives.

2. God's Continued Mercy

The next stop on our tour of verse 6 is a look at the hope of God's mercy, which will also follow us all the days of our lives. "Surely... [God's] *mercy* shall follow me all the days of my life." *Mercy* (or the wonderful, quaint word *loving-kindness*) is David's word for God's tender affection. In the ancient world *mercy* meant "love that flows, not out of a sense of duty, but from deep emotion." David is proclaiming God's steadfast love, and His love even reaches out to those who are unworthy and undeserving.

⁓Building Your Confidence in Him ⁓

The life of Rahab offers us one of God's most dramatic portrayals of His mercy against a background of sin. Rahab was a woman who gave every reason to be shunned and condemned by God and His people. She

was a harlot, a prostitute. Yet she'd heard of God, feared
the Lord, hid His spies, misdirected her king's soldiers,
and helped the Lord's men escape the city and death.
Before the spies from the army of Israel ran for their
lives, they promised this dear woman who had risked
her life that they would spare her and all her family
when they came to conquer the land (Joshua 2).

Did Rahab, a blatant sinner and pagan, deserve to
be spared? Did this woman who had broken God's
holy laws merit a drop of God's grace? Did she warrant
any special treatment or consideration from God and
His people?

No.

And, my friend, neither do we. That's what makes
Rahab's story so beautiful and touching. God says, "All
have sinned and fall short of the glory of God (Romans
3:23). And "the wages of sin is death" (Romans 6:23).

God, in His great mercy, extended His loving-kindness to the undeserving and unworthy sinner Rahab.
In His compassion and grace, He saved her and her
family, turning her dark life and sinful past into an
exquisite cameo of shining faith. Rahab even became
part of the lineage of our Savior, Jesus Christ!

Are you a child of God? In other words, have you
admitted your sins to a holy God? Have you asked for
His mercy and forgiveness? Have you cried out, "God,
be merciful to me a sinner"? (See Luke 18:13.) If so,
you have the promise and hope of God's mercy! And
it will *surely* follow you all the days of your life. Praise
the goodness and mercy of the Lord!

3. God's Continued Pursuit

"Surely [God's] goodness and mercy shall *follow* me all the days of my life." We easily understand that with the word *follow* David is saying God's goodness and mercy will always be with him. But actually David is taking it even further. A mighty warrior, David draws on his military experience to transform the *follow* into meaning "being chased, being relentlessly pursued." Most of David's adult life was spent being pursued by his enemies and by the enemies of God. In Psalm 23 David puts *follow* to a positive use, conveying that God's goodness and mercy will *pursue* us, will *hound* us, each and every day of our lives, just as it did for David. God wants us to experience His mercy and goodness so we can draw closer to Him!

4. God's Continued Presence

The next "snapshot" on our trip through the awesome verse 6 is of the hope we experience because of the continued presence of the Lord. David says, "Surely goodness and mercy shall follow me *all the days of my life.*"

As David ponders the goodness and mercy of God, he gives them each a personality, a presence. He pictures them as following us, as shadowing us, as attending us, as hounding us. Now he adds "as assuring us." No matter what happens in our lives today, tomorrow, or in all the todays to come, God's mercy and love will be with us—*always* with us! Nothing can ever separate us from God's goodness and mercy.

～ Building Your Confidence in Him ～

There are many illustrations of God's attributes of goodness and mercy. The image and language in the following example really touches my heart...and I hope it will yours too.

These two angels of God—Goodness and Mercy—shall follow and encamp around the pilgrim. The white wings of these messengers of the covenant will never be far away from the journeying child, and the air will often be filled with the music of their comings, and their celestial weapons will glance around him in all the fight, and their soft arms will bear him up over all the rough ways, and up higher at last to the throne.[4]

These are beautiful and comforting words, aren't they? But, dear one, with or without the emotional imagery, we have the sure promise of the presence of God's goodness and mercy forever. God will be with us at dawn, at noonday, in the evening, and through the dark night of each and every day. When you need His strength for your life's work each day, God will be there, extending to you all His goodness and mercy. When you need His support for life's trials, when you move from a green pasture to a dark valley, you can hold tightly to the hope of the promise of God's continual goodness and mercy. And when it's time for you to step across the threshold into the unknown, into "the house of the LORD," God's goodness and mercy will escort and follow you there too. *Surely!*

What a marvelous promise of hope.

*God's promise of hope lights a candle in your heart
and creates a blaze of glorious hope
that dispels doubt about your future.
You face the unknown with the known—
with the extended care of God, your Shepherd,
who is the same yesterday, today, and forever.
Praise His holy name!*

12

God's Home Is Yours... Forever!

And I will dwell in the house of the LORD forever.

PSALM 23:6

In My Father's house are many mansions;
if it were not so, I would have told you.
I go to prepare a place for you...
that where I am, there you may be also.

JOHN 14:2-3

Fireworks on the Fourth of July are so awesome. The finales are electrifying as explosions and sounds fill up the night sky. But better yet is that wonderful moment after the final volley, when the smoke from the gunpowder that ignites the splendid sprays and deafening booms clears away and we gaze at the solid splendor of the heavens. Fireworks are stirring, but they're also man-made and fleeting. But the heavens? God's moon and stars? They are permanent. They are the revealed handiwork of the Lord (Psalm 19:1). They are stable and real. The heavens declare God's glory!

In the final verse of Psalm 23 David turns us away from this life, which the Bible calls "a puff of smoke" and "a vapor that appears for a little time and then vanishes away" (James 4:14 NLT and NKJV). He forces our gaze upward to heaven as he pronounces, "And I will dwell in the house of the LORD forever." Suddenly we're transported into the glory of living eternally with Jesus in heaven!

God's care, and His promise to continue caring for us all the days of our lives on earth can be seen like fireworks—thrilling, exciting, and brilliant. But a home in heaven? An eternal home? A place in the house of the Lord forever? Now *that's* like looking at the blazing heavens after the flashes of fireworks fade away. God's promise of a forever home for us is His most dazzling promise of all!

Three More Reasons for Hope in the Future

And now let's finish our "photo tour" of Psalm 23:6. So far we've explored...

- ⤳ God's continued *goodness*
- ⤳ God's continued *mercy*
- ⤳ God's continued *pursuit*
- ⤳ God's continued *presence*

Having been escorted through *all the days of our life* by God's goodness and mercy, pursuit, and presence, we finally reach the Father's house. At last we step into our eternal dwelling place. We are home at last!

5. Eternal Worship

How David—the shepherd, warrior, and fugitive—longs to be near God! To *dwell* with God *in the house of the Lord* is the paramount desire of his heart. And he wants much more than merely staying in God's guest tent. He yearns to dwell *with* God and to be His forever guest, not just an acquaintance or visitor for a brief stay. David wants to stay with God. He wants to experience the fullness of joy and the constant pleasure of being in the Lord's presence!

What will it be like to dwell in the house of the Lord forever? It will be to worship the Lord of that house...forever. Just as the Levites (who were assigned to serve the Lord in His sanctuary) considered the courts of the Lord to be their true home David too has set his mind and heart there...for then he will be in the house of the Lord forever...where he will worship the Lord forever.

⌒ *Building Your Confidence in Him* ⌒

The words David chooses in verse 6 communicate pure worship! He speaks from his heart to God's (and ours!) and tells us what is important, what consumes his heart and soul and mind—the Lord! In fact, David is preoccupied *with* God. His passion is *for* God. His focus is *on* God. And his gaze is ever upward...to that place where he will one day dwell *with* God and worship Him forever.

Where is *your* gaze fixed, friend? And what is your focus producing? Although I couldn't find who the author of the following psalm is, I found his or her musings and gaze a little too close to home:

The Twenty-third Channel

The TV is my shepherd. My spiritual growth shall want. It maketh me to sit down and do nothing for its name's sake, because it requireth all my spare time. It keepeth me from doing my duty as a Christian, because it presenteth so many good shows that I must see.

It restoreth my knowledge of the things of the world, and keepeth me from the study of God's Word. It leadeth me in the paths of failing to attend the evening church services, and doing nothing in the kingdom of God.

Yea, though I live to be a hundred, I shall keep viewing my TV as long as it will work, for it is my closest companion.

Its sounds and pictures, they comfort me.

It presenteth entertainment before me and keepeth me from doing important things with my family. It fills my head with ideas which differ from those in the Word of God.

Surely, no good thing will come out of my life because of so many wasted hours, and I shall dwell in my regrets and remorse forever.[1]

Again, where is *your* gaze fixed? What do you talk about? Where does your heart dwell? What is your greatest pleasure? The next time you hear yourself chattering about a TV program, the news, the latest "talk" from a talk show, remember your heart is showing.

Join me in turning off the twenty-third channel... and worshiping the Lord instead!

⊷

6. An Eternal Home

Home. "The house of the LORD." The concept of a specific place to dwell has a deeply emotional effect on the heart of every person. Imagine what it meant to David, a shepherd who knew all about the nomadic life. Shepherds were on the move their whole lives, regularly pitching and moving their tents as they rotated through the fields to keep their sheep happy and the land healthy.

David's life was a pilgrimage, a journey home. He traveled through many fair meadows and dark valleys. He had his share of storms and adversaries. But God, the Good Shepherd, never failed to care for him. In Psalm 23:7 David reveals he's ready for his troubled trek to end. He's ready to go home!

What did David mean by "the house of the LORD"? We know he's not referring to the Jewish temple in Jerusalem because it wasn't built yet. And it wasn't the house David wished to build for the Lord because he uses the word "forever," and no man-made house lasts that long.

No, David must be referring to something far greater than a building. A forever fellowship with Jehovah beyond the grave. David was a king—and a wealthy one at that. And he possessed worldly riches and had access to any pleasure. But these worldly pursuits didn't—and couldn't!—compare with the eternal pleasure of being at home in the house of the LORD...living with the Lord of the house forever!

⟶ *Building Your Confidence in Him* ⟶

I well remember wrestling with my emotions when our daughter Katherine graduated from college and wanted to live in an apartment with a group of her college friends. *Why?* I argued with myself. *Why would she want to live with a group of young women when*

*her own home, the place where she belongs, is only eight
minutes away? What's wrong with living here?*

But Katherine was 22 years old, and the move was
an obvious next step on her way to independence
and maturity. So off she went to an environment that
turned out to be a blessing. She learned how to cook
for others on a regular basis, to keep her part of the
apartment clean, to enhance her side of the bedroom
with her things, and to get along with others on a
day-in day-out basis.

But I'll never forget Katherine's words the day she
moved back home as she prepared for her wedding.
She sank into the sofa with a sigh and exhaled, "Mom,
it's OK out there, but it's just not *home!*"

I think Katherine's sentiment is what David is telling
us: "It's OK out here (in the world, in the marketplace,
in our friendships, in our experiences, in managing our
challenges), but it's just not *home!*" We yearn to be in
a permanent, loving family, not just guests or people
passing through momentary situations and relation-
ships. And that's what our forever home means to us!
May our hearts ever reflect this truth as we contemplate
the hope we have of an eternal home where we dwell
with the Lord forever.

⤳⤳⤳

7. Eternal Presence

There's no doubt that David broke a barrier when he penned the
sentence, "I will dwell in the house of the LORD forever." Reaching
out with his heart toward the God whose eternal presence he so

longed to enjoy, David touched a higher truth. As one person noted, "There was something else beyond the sunset and evening star."[2] There was an eternal presence. There was God!

Just like David, you and I have conditions in our lives that make the promise of a forever home in the presence of God something we look forward to. As we suffer on earth—dealing with pain, affliction, deprivations, persecutions, and death—we too long to be in God's eternal presence in the house of the Lord...*forever.* Our earthly trials make the promise of heaven so sweet!

What awaits us there? What will we experience when we step across the threshold between earth and heaven? The writer of the book of Revelation tells us that God will be there. And He will "wipe away every tear from [our] eyes; there shall be no more death, nor sorrow, nor crying; and there shall be no more pain" (21:4).

Imagine! No more tears, sadness, enemies, trials, affliction, pain of heart, pain of body, wandering, climbing, trekking, and wading through life. All that we suffer from will be removed...for good. And all that we yearn for will be provided totally. What glory! What peace! Oh, what an existence it will be to dwell in the eternal presence of the Lord!

∼*Building Your Confidence in Him* ∼

The famous preacher D.L. Moody obviously thought much about stepping into the presence of God. He jotted these notes in the margin of his Bible beside Psalm 23:

> For short sorrow, we shall have
> eternal joy.
> For a little hunger, an eternal
> banquet.

For a little sickness and affliction,
    everlasting health and salvation.
For a little bondage, endless liberty.
For disgrace, glory.
For evil surroundings, the elect.
For Satan's temptations, the comfort
    of God.[3]

Our hearts hunger for the fulfillment of the promise of heaven too. We long to worship the Lord...forever, to be at home with Him...forever, to enjoy His presence...forever.

So why don't we worship Him and enjoy His presence right here and now? On earth? Today...and every day? I know we're busy. Every woman is. And I know we're bombarded on every side with distractions and responsibilities. But let's do as David decided to do, "I have set the LORD always before me" (Psalm 16:8).

~ Building Your Confidence in Him ~

What does it mean to "set the Lord always before us"? I once read about a church youth leader who took her youth group on an outing to the Huntington Art Museum in Pasadena, California, to view the fine arts on display. Once there she intently whisked her group from room to room, from painting to painting, from display to display. She was determined her group would see every item in the exhibits. Each time she crisscrossed the museum on the run, she caught sight of one particular room where a gentleman was seated on a bench. He was gazing at one painting. While she and her class were zipping through every nook and cranny of the vast building, this man never moved from his spot. He remained on that bench the entire time the class was there, drinking in the glory of one masterpiece.

With her goal of touring the museum and its legendary gardens accomplished, the church leader breathlessly rounded up the group to bustle them out to the waiting bus. And sure enough, as she went by that one room again, she caught sight of the man. He was still there. As the bus bumped its way home after an exhausting day, she thought about the man. *Yes,* she concluded, *his is the better way.* Admitting that she could hardly recall what she'd seen on her whirlwind tour, she could only imagine what the unknown man was taking home with him—the colors, the details, the understanding, the treasure, the appreciation, the comprehension, the feelings of the famous work of art.

～☆～

What a lesson! Why don't you and I do what this wise man did? Let's put aside the busyness and bustle of life—at least for a specific time each day—and set the Lord before us? Why don't we set the *many things* in life aside and enjoy the *one main Person?* Why don't we choose to sit and soak in God's beauty, God's essence, God's majesty, God's promises, and God's glory...*today...right now?*

When you and I make this daily decision to set the Lord before us, we'll be able to join the writer who yearned for his promised home and wrote the heart song of Psalm 84:

How lovely is Your tabernacle,
O LORD of hosts!
My soul longs, yes, even faints
For the courts of the LORD;
My heart and my flesh cry out for
the living God (verses 1-2).

——————※——————

God's care for you all along the way and
His promise to care for you all the days
of your life are like fireworks—
thrilling, exciting, brilliant.
But a home in heaven?
An eternal home?
A place in the house of the Lord...forever?
Now that's like looking at the blazing heavens
after the flashes of fireworks fade away!

——————※——————

Your Quiet Confidence

One psalm. Six verses. Twelve powerful promises. One hundred and seventeen words. All truly awesome! I pray that you've thought much about all that God is and all that He promises—and does—for you. You, dear fellow traveler, have the Good Shepherd watching over and tending to every detail of your life.

And now, before we leave these sacred words, I want to share with you one of my former pastor's favorite stories about Psalm 23.

In a church meeting one evening, the pastor had those who were visiting stand up and introduce themselves. The first to rise and give his name mentioned that he was an actor.

Thinking quickly, the pastor asked, "Do you know Psalm 23?"

"Why, yes," the actor replied with a smile.

"Would you mind treating our congregation to a recitation of it?"

"I would love to!" came his enthusiastic answer.

Rising in his place the actor turned, acknowledged his audience, cleared his throat, paused, and then launched into a flawless and eloquent oration of the familiar psalm.

When he finished, the people in the church burst into hearty applause. It was perfect. And with such expression.

Before the pastor moved on to the next visitor, he thanked the actor and remarked, "It's obvious you know Psalm 23 well."

The next visitor to introduce himself was elderly and bent with age. He commented that he was a retired preacher.

"Oh! Then I'm sure you know Psalm 23 too!" exclaimed the pastor. "Why don't you share your rendition with our people?"

With great difficulty the old man of God rose from his seat, turned, and with a raspy, aged, shaking voice began. Slowly he articulated his way through the beloved psalm. More than once he had to stop as he struggled with his tears. When he finally finished and sank into his seat, there was only the sound of sniffles as everyone sat too stunned to move or respond.

Dabbing his eyes and finding his voice, the pastor of the church quietly spoke, "And you, sir…it's obvious you know *the Shepherd* well."

A Final Prayer for You

As we go our separate ways, my prayer is that you know the Shepherd well. As we've gone through Psalm 23, I hope you move beyond the poetry and imagery and sentiments to believe and embrace more deeply God's powerful promises to you for each and every circumstance and season of your life. This poem inspires me...and it may encourage you too:

> God is before me, He will be my guide;
> God is behind me, no ill can betide;
> God is beside me, to comfort and cheer;
> God is around me, so why should I fear?

May you know full well and acknowledge with full confidence "the Lord is *my* Shepherd."

Questions and Insights for Deeper Understanding and Discussion

God Is Your Confidence, Hope, and Joy

Psalm 23

1. What truth is taught and what promise is made in Psalm 23:4 regarding all the seasons, years, even the minutes, of your life?

2. How are you comforted or encouraged that the Lord promises to be "with" you through all the seasons of life (Psalm 23:4)?

3. On the presence of God, what did David, the inspired writer of Psalm 23, also say in Psalm 16:8? What does Isaiah 43:2 say on the same subject? And Isaiah 41:10?

God is with you! At every point, every season, every moment, He is with you.

David, the Psalmist

When I'm deciding whether or not to purchase a book, I always read the backcover copy or the book's dust jacket. I want to know what qualifies the author to write on the subject matter. Knowing something about the author also helps me better understand that person's approach and work.

So let's find out about David, the person God used to bring us Psalm 23 with its many marvelous promises. Check out the scriptures listed to see what God tells us about David.

1. Where was David when Samuel came to anoint him to be king (1 Samuel 16:11)?

   ≈ Where was he when Saul needed a musician (16:19)?

   ≈ And where was he when his father needed him to take supplies to his brothers (17:20)?

2. David was probably a teenager when he faced Goliath. How did his experience as a shepherd help him fight the giant (17:34-36)?

   ≈ What shepherd implements did David use against Goliath (17:40)?

3. When God called David to lead His people, what did He say to him (2 Samuel 5:2)? And in 2 Samuel 7:8?

4. Describe David's leadership role according to Psalm 78:70-72.

We learned about David's seasons of youth, maturity, and leadership. But we also discovered that David's faith in a great God carried him through...

> ...a season of rejection
>
> ...a season of fear
>
> ...a season of discouragement
>
> ...a season of disappointment
>
> ...a season of heartbreak

1. How does David's great faith in God encourage and strengthen you in your seasons? Jot down specifics.

   ⋙ How do David's *great failures* encourage and instruct you in your seasons? Again, jot down specifics.

2. How do you think David's early career as a shepherd shaped and prepared him to lead God's people?

❧ Can you think of ways that God has used your past to shape your present? (And have you thanked Him?)

3. How did the prophet Samuel describe David (1 Samuel 13:14; see also Acts 13:22)?

❧ What do you think it means to be "a woman after God's own heart"? Write it down and make this a matter of prayer.

David was a man of great faith, but he was also a man of great failure. And beloved, this is true of everyone!

4. How are you handling your failures? Do you need to admit any past or current sins?

5. What did David say happens when you and I (and David!) admit our sins (Psalm 51:3,7-14)? Why not make a list of your sins and talk to God about them right now?

6. Or maybe you've suffered. How does God help His children when they suffer?

Read the sobering scene described in 2 Samuel 12:13-20 and David's efforts to go on.

7. What steps can you take today to rise up and go on after any disobedience or hard times?

   ⚓ How does Philippians 3:13-14 help you?

   ⚓ And how about 2 Corinthians 4:8-9?

   ⚓ And Philippians 4:13?

1

God Cares for You

The Bible contains many references to God as our Shepherd. In fact, the phrase "the Lord is my shepherd" is a name of God—*Jehovah-Rohi*. Let's look at more descriptive scriptures.

Jehovah-Rohi Feeds, Leads, and Warns

1. In Psalm 74:1 how does the psalmist view God's people?

2. In Psalm 77:20 How does the psalmist view God's guidance?

   ≫ Who were two of God's shepherds?

3. In Psalm 78:52-53 how does the psalmist view God's people?

   ≫ And God's guidance?

4. In Psalm 79:13 how does the psalmist view God's people?

5. In Psalm 80:1 how does the psalmist address God?

6. Look at Isaiah 40:11. What role and actions does Isaiah ascribe to God?

7. In John 10:11-16 and 26-28 who is speaking?

    ⚘ How does He refer to Himself (verses 11 and 14)?

8. In Hebrews 13:20 how is Jesus referred to?

    ⚘ And in 1 Peter 2:25?

    ⚘ In 1 Peter 5:4?

    ⚘ In Revelation 7:17?

9. What new assurances do you enjoy when you realize Jesus is your Shepherd?

10. According to John 10, verses 4, 5, 14, 27, and 28, what are the characteristics of Jesus' sheep?

Your Moment with the Shepherd

Now that you know more about the role of a good shepherd and his care for his sheep think about how the Good Shepherd feeds you.

1. How's your appetite for God's food—for His Word?

    ∾ Describe your times in God's Word—in God's green pastures—this past week.

    ∾ Do you need to make any adjustments in your "feeding" habits? If yes, what are they?

2. How can you alter your daily schedule to allow more time to feed on God's Word?

3. How is your willingness to follow *Jehovah-Rohi?* Do you need to change anything? If yes, what will you do?

4. Is there anything God is asking of you today that you are failing to heed and follow? Are there any adjustments you need to make in your "following" habits?

Jehovah-Rohi warns us because He wants the best for us.

5. Are any warning lights flashing in your life? Are you playing life too close to the edge? Are you dabbling in areas of sin? Do you need to change anything?

6. Are you partaking of things God explicitly warns you against? Are you involved in any activities that aren't honoring or pleasing God? If so, what are you going to do?

7. Are there any adjustments you need to make in your "listening" habits? Does anything need to be eliminated from your life? Please explain.

8. Think on the beautiful description of God in Isaiah 40:11. What are the fears you face today? How do these words about God's care "comfort you" (as Isaiah 40:1 says)?

9. Look again at your answers from John 10. As you consider the behaviors that characterize the sheep that follow Jesus, which ones are you doing well? Are there any that need work?

   ～ Read the descriptions of the restless and discontent sheep, the worldling sheep, and the devoted sheep. Which of these sheep most closely resemble you? Do you have any corrections to make in your "following" habits? What are they?

⤫ Write out a plan of action and a prayer of commitment to be a more devoted follower.

10. What was the sacrifice of the Good Shepherd on your behalf (John 10:11,15)?

⤫ In view of Jesus' willingness to make the sacrifice, what steps will you take to be a more committed and obedient follower?

How blessed we are to have a God who cares about us, His women, and to have the care of our God! The extent of God's promise to care for His own is immeasurable, unsearchable, and fathomless. Read the list of some of God's care of and for you. Look up these powerful promises in your Bible and memorize them. And don't forget to thank *Jehovah-Rohi!*

⤫ God will "keep" you as the apple of His eye (Psalm 17:8).

⤫ He will "keep" you in all your ways (Psalm 91:11).

⤫ He will "keep" you in perfect peace (Isaiah 26:3).

⤫ He will "keep" that which you have committed to Him against that day (2 Timothy 1:12).

⤫ He will "keep" you from the hour of temptation

and support you in the time of trial (1 Corinthians 10:13).

✎ He will "keep" you from falling (Jude 24).

✎ He will "keep" you as a shepherd cares for his flock of sheep (Jeremiah 31:10).[1]

2

God Will Always Provide

One of my favorite Christian songs is "All That I Need Is All That You Are." Not only is the song lovely and the lyrics inspiring, but the title seems to say it all when it comes to the person of God and His provision for our needs.

As we think about the essential needs in life, it's comforting to have the promise of God's provision so that we may confidently declare, "I shall not want," and realize that all that we need is all that He is. God's provision for us illustrates another character trait of the Lord as revealed in His name *Jehovah-Jireh*, "The Lord will provide."

Meet Jehovah-Jireh

1. Quickly read through Genesis 22:1-14, which tells the story of *Jehovah-Jireh*.

    ≫ Who are the principal people (verses 1 and 2)?

    ≫ What was God's command (verse 2)?

    ≫ What was the problem (verse 7)?

    ≫ What answer was given (verse 8)?

≈ What was God's solution (verse 13)?

≈ What name was given to the place where this occurred (verse 14)?

2. Both Abraham and his wife, Sarah, had a long history of trusting God...and of learning to trust God. Hebrews 11 has been given such titles as "The Saints' Hall of Fame," "The Honor Roll of Old Testament Saints," and "Heroes of Faith."[2] Note the instances and the details of faith in God as revealed in...

≈ Abraham in Hebrews 11:8-10—

≈ Sarah in Hebrews 11:11—

≈ Abraham and Sarah's offspring in Hebrews 11:12-13—

≈ Abraham in Hebrews 11:17-19—

3. Now that we've noted the faith of Sarah, read about her encounter with the Lord in Genesis 18:1-15. What announcement did the Lord make in verse 10?

≈ And what was Sarah's response (verses 10-15)?

⟹ And why (verses 11-13)?

⟹ What searing question did the Lord ask Sarah—and you!—in verse 14?

4. What is said of Abraham's faith in Romans 4:20-21?

God Provides

1. Did you catch what the apostle Paul said in Romans 4 about Abraham's faith in "the promises of God"? Look at these scriptures and note the promises made and the conditions for them.

                              Promise   *Condition*

   ⟹ Psalm 34:9—

   ⟹ Psalm 34:10—

   ⟹ Psalm 84:11—

2. Truly God promises to meet the needs of His people! Note several more instances of God's provision in these verses:

   ⟹ Deuteronomy 2:7—How long had God met His people's needs?

❧ Deuteronomy 8:7—What did God promise His people in the Promised Land?

Your Moment with the Shepherd

1. Jot down what you consider to be the primary necessities in life.

   Now write down the promise from Psalm 23:1.

   ❧ For an additional blessing look again at the remainder of Psalm 23. List the many "needs" God promises to meet.

2. *Jehovah-Jireh!* Think back on the command God gave to Abraham in Genesis 22:2. What do you think you would have done?

3. Look back at Sarah's encounter with the Lord in Genesis 18. As you think about your faith in God and your responses to your problems and to His promises, what answer are you exhibiting in response to God's question, "Is anything too hard for the Lord?"

   ❧ If you're facing a seemingly impossible situation now, how does the thought of *Jehovah-Jireh,* "the Lord will provide," encourage you?

3

God Gives You Rest

The Place of Rest

1. Quickly note how these references describe "green pastures."

    ⤷ Deuteronomy 32:2—

    ⤷ 2 Samuel 23:4—

    ⤷ Proverbs 27:25—

    ⤷ How do these conditions contribute to the sheep's rest?

2. What is pictured in the images of these scriptures that refer to physical "resting places" of sheep, camels, and people?

    ⤷ 2 Samuel 7:8 through Isaiah 65:10—

    ⤷ Ezekiel 25:5—

    ⤷ Isaiah 32:18—

The Plan for Rest

1. According to Exodus 20:10, what is God's purpose for the Sabbath?

2. Jesus knew of our need for rest and planned for it. How does Mark 6:30-32 reveal this?

3. What do these verses indicate about Jesus' physical needs?

     ᴥ Mark 4:38—

     ᴥ John 4:6—

The Procedure for Rest

1. According to Psalm 23:2, what is God's procedure for ensuring rest for His own?

2. The prophet Elijah was one of God's choice servants who was assigned by God to prophesy a long, extended drought to King Ahab (1 Kings 17:1). When Elijah next saw King Ahab, it resulted in a showdown between God and His representative, Elijah, and the priests of Baal (1 Kings 18:20-40). At this point, Queen Jezebel threatened Elijah's life, and he ran away. Now read 1 Kings 19.

↘ How distraught was Elijah (verses 1-5)?

↘ How did God minister to Elijah (verses 5-6)?

↘ And how did He minister to him again (verse 7)?

↘ What was the result of Elijah's rest and God's provision and care for him (verse 8)?

↘ How else did God tend to and encourage His faithful, tired prophet (verses 9-21)?

Your Moment with the Shepherd

1. Take a minute to think about the times when you need rest. What is your mental condition?

↘ And your physical condition?

↘ And your spiritual condition?

↘ How does a time of resting in the presence of the Lord refresh you?

2. Think about the three conditions that interfere with the rest every woman needs—fear, hunger, and fighting. How do these promises, assurances, and instructions contribute to your rest and peace?

Fear

🖎 Consider Isaiah 41:10. How does God promise to fortify you?

🖎 What does God promise in these verses?
  • Joshua 1:9—

  • Deuteronomy 31:6—

  • Exodus 33:14—

  • Psalm 3:5 and 4:8—

Hunger

"God's ordinances are the green pastures in which food is provided for all believers; the word of life is the nourishment of the new man. It is milk for babes, pasture for sheep...a green pasture for faith to feed in."[3]

⤚ Do a heart check: Answer the following questions and if improvement is needed, note what you're going to do.

    ⤚ Do you consider your times in God's Word a *necessity?*

    ⤚ Do you enjoy the nourishment of God's Word *regularly?*

    ⤚ Is your appetite for God's Word *increasing?*

    ⤚ Which stage best describes your times in God's Word: cod liver oil stage, shredded wheat stage, or peaches and cream stage?

Fighting

⤚ Describe your internal emotions and their physical effects on you when you're involved in an argument, quarrel, or dispute, or when you witness these between others.

⤚ How does the elimination or solution of the problem bring rest?

3. Does it comfort you to know that the Lord "makes" you lie down in green pastures and rest? In your life, think of times God made you rest. How did He provide it? What were the results?

4. "Waiting" can become one of God's opportunities for rest for His busy and breathless and sometimes beat-up sheep. How do you think waiting causes you to grow in patience?

   ⚘ How do you think waiting creates an opportunity to learn to trust the Lord?

   ⚘ How do you think waiting causes you to grow in patience?

   ⚘ How do you think waiting encourages and creates greater fellowship with God?

   ⚘ How do you think waiting will energize you for the day...or days...ahead?

   ⚘ What can you do today to "lie down" in God's "green pastures" and experience His promised rest?

4

God's Peace Is Always Available to You

Our Shepherd knows our need for peace. He promises to lead us to places, such as still waters, to ensure that we drink in, take in, and bask in His peace.

1. Note how these scriptures show how the Lord leads us:

    ⚘ Psalm 77:20—

    ⚘ Isaiah 40:11—

    ⚘ Isaiah 49:10—

The Still Waters

1. There's no doubt that every woman has a need for peace as she lives her busy life in a hectic world. However, throughout time God's people have found their "still waters," their "place," for tapping into God's peace. Note the places (or Person) where these people of God found peace.

    ⚘ Abraham (Genesis 19:27)—

⇜ David (Psalm 32:7)—

⇜ The psalmist (Psalm 119:114)—

⇜ Daniel (Daniel 6:10)—

⇜ Mary (Luke 10:39)—

⇜ Jesus (Mark 1:35)—

⇜ Jesus (Luke 22:39-41)—

Meet Jehovah-Shalom and Gideon

1. *Jehovah-Shalom!* Quickly read through Judges 6:11-24.

   ⇜ How did the Angel of the Lord greet Gideon (verse 12)?

   ⇜ What did the Angel of the Lord ask of Gideon (verse 14)?

   ⇜ Why was Gideon so disturbed (verse 15)?

⚜ How did the Lord calm Gideon's fears (verse 16)?

⚜ What caused Gideon to fear for his life again (verse 22)?

⚜ And what was the Lord's answer (verse 23)?

⚜ And how did Gideon commemorate this encounter with God (verse 24)?

More About the Shepherd

1. God's peace is promised to you in the New Testament. What new information do you learn from these verses?

   ⚜ John 14:27—

   ⚜ Romans 5:1—

   ⚜ 1 Corinthians 14:33—

   ⚜ 2 Thessalonians 3:16—

2. Did you relate to the story of my friend and her struggle with "the four **A**'s"? Look at what God's Word says about each of the "**A**'s." While you work through this exercise, ask your heart if there is anything you're failing to do to follow God.

   ⚮ **An**ything (Acts 9:6)—

   ⚮ **An**ywhere (Isaiah 6:8)—

   ⚮ **An**y time (Matthew 2:13-14)—

   ⚮ **At** any cost (Philippians 3:7-8)—

3. How does Abraham's obedience to God in Genesis 12:1 and 4 demonstrate the four **A**'s?

Meet the Prince of Peace

1. Have you made a "transaction" with *Jehovah-Shalom,* the Prince of Peace? If so, recount briefly how you became a Christian.

⚬ If you haven't, why not? Do you want to do it now? Then ask God by praying this prayer or something similar.

Lord, I want to be Your child, a woman after Your heart. I want to live my life in You, and through You, and for You. I acknowledge my sins and shortcomings, my failure to live up to Your standards. I received Your Son, Jesus Christ, into my heart, giving thanks that He died on the cross for my sins. Thank You for giving me Your grace and Your strength so that I can follow You wholeheartedly. Amen.

2. What hurdle are you facing? And what fears do you have regarding the future?

   ⚬ How does it encourage you to know that the Lord, your Good Shepherd, leads you every step of the way through life?

   ⚬ How does it encourage you to know that God leads you to places of peace "beside still waters"?

   ⚬ How does the fact that the Lord is with you strengthen your courage and give you peace to face what you know is coming...and what you don't know is coming?

3. Do you have a time and a place where you retreat regularly to commune with the God of peace? Describe them.

   ⚬ My time is...

✒ My place is…

4. As you think about the four **A**'s, is there any area in your life where you are failing to follow God's leading? Can you pinpoint why? Are you afraid? Worried? Anxious? Disobedient? Are there fears? Worries? Anxieties?

   ✒ Ask God to give you His strength to commit to follow Him as He leads you so that you may experience His perfect peace.

5. After learning more about God's promise of peace, can you think of any instance when you should not enjoy God's peace? Please explain.

   ✒ How do you plan to use the truths learned in this lesson to fight against fear or worry and gain God's peace? Be specific.

Isn't it reassuring to have the promise of God's peace? How *could* we, as busy women, make it through life—even through one day!— without it? But God is faithful to lead us to a place of peace, at least in our hearts, if not in our surroundings. God's peace is promised and available…if we would but follow our Shepherd. So, dear one, *walk* with God. Then you will experience God's peace!

5

God Is Your Healer

What woman doesn't need her soul restored? And what woman doesn't need her spirit healed? Do you ever feel the need for a spiritual repair job? Take heart! Your Shepherd sees your need.

1. According to Hebrew scholars, the restoration of the "soul" in Psalm 23:3 means the rekindling or quickening of the exhausted spirit. Look up in a dictionary a few meanings of *restore* and jot them down.

2. Now that you have a better idea of the concept of restoration, what needs are revealed in these verses?

   ❧ Psalm 19:7—

   ❧ Psalm 23:3—

   ❧ Psalm 51:12—

   ❧ Psalm 147:3—

   ❧ Isaiah 61:1—

✎ Jeremiah 3:22—

✎ Jeremiah 27:22—

✎ Jeremiah 30:17—

✎ Galatians 6:1—

The Character of Jehovah-Rophe

1. *Jehovah-Rophe,* meaning "Jehovah heals," teaches us more about God's ministry of healing and restoration. What great event in Israel's history is told in Exodus 14:27-31?

   ✎ How did the Israelites respond (15:1)?

   ✎ According to 15:22-23, what was the first trial God's people faced in the wilderness?

   ✎ And how did they respond (verse 24)?

   ✎ What was God's solution (verse 25)?

ᴥ List the four requirements God laid out for His people in verse 26.

ᴥ What did God promise to do if these four conditions were met?

ᴥ How does God refer to Himself in verse 26?

The Case of Elijah

1. As we've already learned, Elijah was one of God's cast-down sheep. List "The Course of Restoration":

    ᴥ Stage 1—

    ᴥ Stage 2—

    ᴥ Stage 3—

2. Read again 1 Kings 19. Note these three stages of restoration in Elijah's cast-down condition. How did God "heal" and restore His beloved prophet and servant?

    ᴥ Stage 1—

ᕯ Stage 2—

ᕯ Stage 3—

More About the Shepherd

1. God's restoration is also emphasized in the New Testament. List God's concerns for the saints in these verses. Notice that the emphasis is on spiritual restoration rather than on physical restoration.

   ᕯ Paul's prayer in Ephesians 1:15-18—

   ᕯ Paul's prayer in Ephesians 3:14-19—

   ᕯ Paul's prayer in Philippians 1:9-11—

   ᕯ Paul's prayer in Colossians 1:9-12—

   ᕯ John's greeting to Gaius in 3 John 2—

Your Moment with the Shepherd

1. In general, how do you respond to physical or emotional testing?

    ⤲ What spiritual responses does God desire from you, regardless of your physical condition?

2. As you think about God's promise in Psalm 23:3 to heal and restore your broken heart and crushed spirit and to bind up your wounds (see Psalm 147:3), what better response will you give to testing in the future?

3. What encouragement do you receive from God's restoration of His prophet Elijah in 1 Kings 19:4-15?

    ⤲ And what practical lessons do you learn from taking care of your physical and spiritual condition?

    ⤲ About ministering to others?

4. What actions can you take to ensure spiritual health and healing in…

    ⤲ feeding on God's Word?

✒ communing with God through prayer?

5. Jot down a plan of action that will help you look to God to rekindle and quicken your soul the next time you are down or discouraged or suffering physically.

Healing. Just hearing the word we immediately think of physical healing. Physical health is definitely important, especially when it's deteriorating. But how encouraging to know that God is more concerned for our spiritual health, and He promises to strengthen us spiritually for the physical trials that will most assuredly come our way. Though outwardly we are wearing down and wasting away, inwardly we are being restored and renewed day by day (2 Corinthians 4:16).

Dear one, rather than giving up or giving in to weakness, weariness, and depression, let us look up—up to God and to His high and treasured promises. Let God give us His promised strength to deal with the inevitable and trust Him to work out the impossible.

6

God Will Guide You

God not only leads us as His women beside His still waters and restores our souls, He promises to guide us in the paths of righteousness.

As a child of God (and a sheep of the Shepherd!), your desire is to follow His guidance. What do you learn from these scriptures about that desire?

1. What does the psalmist cry out for in Psalm 16:11?

   ⮕ And in Psalm 27:11?

2. What does the psalmist say will help him stay on the path (Psalm 119:105)?

The "Paths"

1. The word "path" is also translated "way" in the Bible. What do you learn from these verses?

   ⮕ Proverbs 12:15—

   ⮕ Proverbs 31:27—

⟁ Isaiah 30:21—

⟁ Isaiah 55:8-9—

The God of Righteousness

1. Our Shepherd faithfully guides us, but we have choices to make about following. What do these references teach you about following the Shepherd's guidance?

    ⟁ Psalm 119:30—

    ⟁ Psalm 119:59-60—

    ⟁ Proverbs 3:6—

2. Read Proverbs 4:14-15. List the six specific instructions God gives us for walking in righteousness and staying on His righteous path.

3. Now read Proverbs 4:23-27 and 23:19. Itemize the specific instructions God gives us in each verse for walking in righteousness and staying on His righteous path.

The Purpose of God's Guidance

1. According to Psalm 23:3, why does God guide us in the paths of righteousness?

2. *Jehovah-Tsidkenu* means "the Lord our righteousness" and reveals the righteousness of God to us and His standard of righteousness. As we look into the history of this name of God, we learn that God's people continually sinned against Him for 100 years before being taken captive. Obviously they needed help in meeting God's standard. What was God's solution (Jeremiah 23:5-6)?

   ⮬ What promise from God would this future event fulfill (2 Samuel 7:16)?

More About the Shepherd

1. As New Testament believers we receive help from God to walk in His paths of righteousness. What do you learn from these scriptures about how God helps us?

   ⮬ John 16:13—

   ⮬ Galatians 6:1—

   ⮬ James 1:5—

✻ Hebrews 13:17—

Your Moment with the Shepherd

1. Evaluate "the path" of your life. Are you walking in God's "stiff and straight" path of righteousness? Explain.

   ✻ Are there any areas where you have strayed off the path of righteousness?

2. List the seven A's that quickly turn our bad habits and wrong ways into a righteous walk.

   ✻ Which of these areas are you weak in? Check or circle them, explain, and write down what you'll do to remedy any problems.

3. We are constantly bombarded by other voices. According to Scripture, what are some of these influences?

   ✻ 1 Corinthians 15:33—

   ✻ Galatians 5:16—

⋙ 1 John 2:15—

4. Are you listening to voices other than God's? Explain.

5. Now look at Psalm 119:30. God *promises* to guide you. Do you need to spend more time in His Word looking at His "stiff and straight" ordinances and being guided by Him?

   ⋙ What plan of action can you make...and take to improve in this area?

6. "For His name's sake" is an important reason God guides us. How does this relate to you and your family? How can you more rigorously guard your family's reputation? How can you more faithfully watch over the ways—the paths—of your loved ones (Proverbs 31:27)?

   ⋙ What can you do today to be more careful to guard your Shepherd's name and reputation?

7. Check the "heart check" questions at the end of this chapter in the main text. Then pray along with David in Psalm 139:23-24 and search your heart:

Search me, O God, and know my heart;
Try me, and know my anxieties;
And see if there is any wicked way in me,
And lead me in the way everlasting.

⚓ What must you do to benefit from God's promise to guide you as you obediently follow Him?

My friend, it doesn't matter *where* God is leading and guiding you. It only matters that *He* is your Guide, and that He *is* leading you in *His* paths of righteousness!

7

God Never Leaves You

Our walk through God's promises turns from green pastures, still waters, and paths of righteousness to the valley of the shadow of death. God's promises will assist us in this new path we travel with Him.

The Way of the Path

1. Note how the Bible uses "the valley of the shadow of death" and any other descriptive words used with "shadow of death."

    ✒ Job 3:5—darkness, cloud, blackness

    ✒ Job 10:21-22—

    ✒ Job 16:16—

    ✒ Job 24:17—

    ✒ Job 28:3—

    ✒ Job 34:22—

≽ Job 38:17—

≽ Psalm 44:19—

≽ Psalm 107:10 and 14—

≽ Jeremiah 2:6—

≽ Jeremiah 13:16—

2. In ten words or less, summarize the meaning of "shadow of death."

Walk in the Path

1. Psalm 23 is full of peaceful, pastoral imagery. But leading sheep was a dangerous profession. David knew what it was like to walk daily with the sheep. What did he experience along the way (1 Samuel 17:34-36)?

2. In Genesis 31:38-40 Jacob details what it was like to shepherd the flocks of Laban. What were some of the dangers and drudgeries?

3. Describe the gruesome scene pictured in Amos 3:12.

4. According to Luke 2:8, what was another duty of shepherds?

More About the Shepherd

1. Even with the dangers of the shadow of death, why was the psalmist not afraid (Psalm 23:4)?

2. What do these Old Testament scriptures reveal about the promise of God's presence?

   ⤳ Deuteronomy 31:6—

   ⤳ Joshua 1:9—

   ⤳ Psalm 46:1-2—

   ⤳ Isaiah 41:10—

3. The New Testament is also filled with promises of the presence of God. What do these scriptures reveal?

   ⤳ Matthew 28:20—

⮾ Acts 18:9-10—

⮾ Hebrews 13:5-6—

Your Moment with the Shepherd

1. Clearly shepherding had its dangers and terrors. Every shepherd and his flock spent time in "the valley of the shadow of death." And so do we. What was the last time you faced a particularly dark and difficult situation? How did the promise of God's presence help you?

2. Is there anything you dread in the future? Why? How can the promise of God's presence dispel your fear?

   ⮾ How does David's famous "I will" from Psalm 23:4 help you with the temptation to fear?

3. Every woman faces trials and tragedies, difficulties and discouragements. In your current difficulty, how are you looking to the Lord, counting on His promised presence, and refusing to fear?

   ⮾ What three commands does Jesus give in John 14:1?

⚞ How are you doing in the Trust Department? What can you do to increase your trust in God and His promises?

⚞ Look again at the promises regarding fear and the presence of God in chapter 3. Which one stands out to you the most? Memorize it...and fear not!

4. What does Jesus say is the role of the Holy Spirit in our lives today (John 14:16-17)?

5. At all times—even in the darkest times—you...

   ...walk by divine appointment

   ...walk in divine presence

   ...walk by divine grace

   ...walk by divine purpose

   ⚞ How can you put these to use in your current hard time? What can you do to remember them for the next time you face difficulties?

It's also true that the more lofty our thoughts about God, the better we are able to cope with the issues of life. Write out how your attitude would improve in your current trials by remembering who God is and His characteristics and promises.

8

God's Comfort Is Only a Prayer Away

Jehovah-Shammah

1. *Jehovah-Shammah,* "Jehovah is there," brings much comfort as we walk with God through life. God promised His presence among His people from the beginning. Note some of the manifestations of His presence:

   ⚹ Exodus 23:20—

   ⚹ Exodus 40:34-38—

   ⚹ 2 Chronicles 7:1-3—

2. Due to the desecration of God's temple by God's people what happened (Ezekiel 10:18)?

3. What is the final promise for the new heaven and earth (Ezekiel 48:35)?

Ezekiel 48:35 says: "the city is called YHWH [Jehovah] Shammah, 'The LORD is there.'" The departed glory of God...has returned...and His dwelling, the temple, is in the very center of the district given over to the Lord. With this final promise, all of the unconditional promises God made to Israel in...

> the Abrahamic Covenant (Genesis 12),
> the Levitic Covenant (Numbers 25),
> the Davidic Covenant (2 Samuel 7), and
> the New Covenant (Jeremiah 31)

have been fulfilled. So this final verse provides the consummation of Israel's history—the returned presence of God![4]

4. Note what these verses say about God's presence.

⤳ Psalm 46:1—

⤳ verses 4-5a—

⤳ verse 7—

⤳ verse 11—

⤳ Psalm 132:13-14—

⤳ Isaiah 12:6—

⚘ Isaiah 63:9—

⚘ Jeremiah 3:17—

Comfort Is There

1. When David acknowledged God's presence in Psalm 34:4, what effect did it have upon him?

2. Who are the people who enjoy God's comfort in Psalm 34:18?

   ⚘ And in Psalm 145:18?

3. As a New Testament believer, you have another source of help and comfort. What Person of God is always present with you according to these scriptures?

   ⚘ John 14:17—

   ⚘ 1 Corinthians 3:16—

   ⚘ 1 Corinthians 6:19—

～ Regarding comfort, what promises, truths, and benefits do you discover in 2 Corinthians 1:3 and 4? (Don't
forget to notice that God's comfort is active, extensive,
purposeful, and specific.)

The Rod and the Staff Are There

1. In addition to God's marvelous presence, you also have the presence of His weapons—His rod and His staff—to comfort you.
Note some of the uses of these two weapons.

～ Genesis 49:10—

～ Exodus 21:19—

～ Leviticus 27:32—

～ 2 Samuel 7:14—

～ 2 Samuel 23:21—

↘ Micah 7:14—

↘ Zechariah 8:4—

As you can readily see, these two implements had a variety of uses. In the imagery of Psalm 23, you can also sense the comfort and confidence the rod and the staff brought to the shepherd and the sheep.

Your Moment with the Shepherd

Comfort! What woman doesn't need it daily? And yet we have all the comfort we need in the presence of God, who is near to all who believe in Him and belong to Him.

1. How does the knowledge of the Shepherd's weapons and His ability to use them on your behalf comfort you? And in what specific situations?

2. How does God use these tools to protect you?

   ↘ To correct you?

   ↘ To guide you?

➤ To dispel your fears?

3. As you think about your day, your week, the year ahead, and the path of the future, how does the promise of God's presence comfort you? After writing out your answer, thank God for His presence and care every day, all the way.

9

God Is Your Friend...
and So Much More

Some say there's nothing like Middle Eastern hospitality. Let's learn a little more about what it meant to be a guest in a Middle Eastern home or tent at the time Psalm 23 was written...and how as one of God's women you can extend hospitality and friendship today.

The Server, the Supply, and the Style

1. Look at the scene of the gracious hosts, Abram and Sarai, in Genesis 18:1-8. Note the preparations they made for their guests. Also write down what is related to the server, what is related to the supply, and what is related to the style.

   ➤ Eagerness (verse 2)—

   ➤ Posture (verse 2)—

   ➤ Attitude (verse 3)—

   ➤ Provision (verse 4)—

   ➤ Menu (verses 6-8)—

⌇ Preparation (verses 6-7)—

⌇ Presentation (verse 8)—

2. Now look in on the scene in Genesis 19:1-3. What similarities do you notice? Again, note the information about the *server,* the *supply,* and the *style.*

⌇ Verse 1—

⌇ Verse 2—

⌇ Verse 3—

3. Consider "the wise woman" from Proverbs 9:1-6. She is a model of hospitality for every woman. What was a part of her work (verse 2)? Once again, what described the server, the supply, and the style?

⌇ What kind of attitude did she exhibit toward hospitality (verse 3)?

4. A few scenes of hospitality and friendship in the Holy Land from

the New Testament reveal the same importance. As usual, pay attention to the *server,* the *supply,* and the *style.*

> ✍ Who extended the loving care and service of hospitality in John 13:2-5?

>> ✍ And to whom?

>> ✍ And in John 21:12-13?

>> ✍ And to whom?

5. Lydia extended hospitality and friendship to many. Who were the recipients of her graciousness in Acts 16:14-15 and 40? What did she offer?

6. Aquila and Priscilla continually opened their hearts and home to others. To whom—and in what ways—did they extend their gracious hospitality and friendship in...

> ✍ Acts 18:1-3—

> ✍ Romans 16:3-5—

> ✍ 1 Corinthians 16:19—

7. Mary, the mother of John Mark, also opened her heart and home to others. To whom and for what purpose, according to Acts 12:12?

8. What does the New Testament say to you in this vital area of hospitality and friendship with other believers?

    ⤜ Romans 12:13—

    ⤜ Hebrews 13:2—

    ⤜ 1 Peter 4:9—

A Sample of Blessings

1. List the ten blessings that are available and that you can enjoy as a child of God. Also note your personal pattern of hospitality toward others. When was the last time someone offered you the blessing of hospitality? What did he or she do?

Your Moment with the Shepherd

1. Think about your family and your opportunities to minister to their physical and spiritual needs at the table. Then read over

the ten blessings characteristic of a visit in the Lord's tent. How do you rate as a server?

⚘ How would you rate your supply? Your style?

⚘ How can you make the time spent at your table more of an intimate feast and a festival of joy?

2. As you take in these warm and generous and gracious instances of friendship to strangers, or "stranger love" (the meaning of hospitality), what do you conclude about hospitality?

⚘ About mealtime?

⚘ About meal preparations?

⚘ Can you think of two or three changes you need to make in the area of hospitality?

3. What blessings do your family and guests experience when they step into your house? Is there more you can do to make them feel welcomed and loved?

Dear sister, I have read countless surveys that identify the Number One problem women face as loneliness. Most of the women who report this as a pressing problem are either single and have no close friends or they are married to husbands who are distant either by design or because of the demands of work.

For a Christian woman, loneliness should be only a fleeting issue. Why? Because we have a friend who is always here—Jesus—whom we can always talk to and visit with.

Think about this: Your hospitality—your open heart and open home—is a way you can extend the care and friendship you enjoy with Jesus to others.

10

God Will Always Protect You

Wasn't it exciting to look at the generous hospitality portrayed in Psalm 23:5? Now let's consider the setting for this gracious provision—"in the presence of my enemies." The host promises his guests protection.

The Situation

1. What was the situation and the setting described for the weary pilgrim's feast in Psalm 23:5?

2. In the book of Ezra we meet Ezra, a godly man preparing for a pilgrimage from Babylon to Jerusalem.

    ⇒ What did he do for protection before beginning his trek (Ezra 8:21)?

    ⇒ Why (verse 22)?

    ⇒ How did God answer Ezra's prayer (verses 23 and 31)?

    ⇒ Those who entered a Middle-Eastern home were promised protection by the host, regardless of cost. Look at

Joshua 2:1-6 and briefly note the host and the guest(s) and the details surrounding their safety.

The Scene

1. Describe the lavish provisions listed in Psalm 23:5.

2. Review the story of Lot's hospitality to his guests in Genesis 19.

   ⟶ Describe Lot's attitude (verse 1).

   ⟶ Describe his invitation (verse 2).

   ⟶ When the angels declined, how did Lot persist (verse 3)?

   ⟶ Once his guests were inside, what did Lot do (verse 3)?

Protection and Security

1. In Lot's hospitality to two angels, what happened after dinner (verse 4)?

⚜ What did the people want (verse 5)?

⚜ What did Lot do about the situation (verses 6-7)?

⚜ In verse 8?

⚜ What next happened to Lot (verse 9)?

⚜ How far was Lot willing to go to protect his guests?

Victory

1. Sometimes a prisoner was chained to the pillars of a palace and forced to "feast" his eyes on a feast celebrating his defeat. In Judges 16:23 who was celebrating?

⚜ How did they celebrate (verse 25)?

Our Savior, Jehovah-Nissi

1. Even when there is no home or host in sight, you have the Lord to protect you from your enemies. This protection is provided by *Jehovah-Nissi*—meaning "Jehovah, my banner." Look at Exodus 17 for the history of this great name of God.

⚞ What is happening in this scene (verse 8)?

⚞ How does Moses respond (verse 9)?

⚞ What is Moses' role (verse 9)?

⚞ How does the battle go (verses 11-12a)?

⚞ And how is the problem solved (verse 12)?

⚞ And what is the result (verse 13)?

⚞ How does Moses respond to this (verse 15)?

2. How do you think Moses interpreted the victory of the Israelites? And why?

3. *Nissi,* or standard, or banner, was a pole with an emblem on top. For a better understanding of the use of a banner, look at Numbers 21.

⚞ What was the problem (verses 5-6)?

⚞ What did God tell Moses to do (verse 8)?

⌇ And what was the result?

⌇ How were those who looked at the banner or bronze-serpent ensign on the pole protected?

More About the Shepherd

1. How do these verses describe some of the many ways God protects you as His dear child?

    ⌇ Proverbs 18:10—

    ⌇ Psalm 3:5 and 4:8—

    ⌇ Psalm 27:1—

    ⌇ Psalm 34:7—

    ⌇ Psalm 121:7-8—

    ⌇ John 10:28-29—

2. God has given you armor. Read Ephesians 6:10-17.

    ⌇ What commands are given to you in verses 10-11?

⤳ What are the six most necessary pieces of spiritual armor God gives His children (verses 14-17)?

God's promises to protect every man and every woman who believes in, belongs to, and obeys Him!

Your Moment with the Shepherd

1. What is your favorite promise from the Bible that reminds you of God's protection? Record the situation that brought it to your mind.

2. When did you experience a victory or "won a battle" in the presence of your enemies because God's banner was over you? Explain.

3. What truths regarding the protective presence of the Lord are revealed in Psalm 139:1-12? Which of these truths mean the most to you...and why?

Does this bring to mind the popular chorus "His Banner over Me Is Love"? What a wonderful protection God's love is! God loved the world and sent His Son (John 3:16). Christ loved the church and died for her (Ephesians 5:25). And Jesus loves me, and nothing can separate me from that love (Romans 8:38-39). What a marvelous protection God's banner of love is for me...and you!

11

God Is Your Hope

In the final verse of Psalm 23, David turns his thinking from what God does and has done for him to what God will do for him forever.

Looking Back...and Up

1. Remember the box I shared about that held the receipts that showed how Jim was taking care of me and planning for my future? Psalm 23 is "the ultimate box" for us. Note all God promises in Psalm 23:1-5 that show He's going to provide for His people.

Moving from Experience to Faith

1. Write down what God promises to provide for His own in the future as noted in Psalm 23:6.

Seven Reasons for Hope in the Future

1. **God's Continued Goodness.** *Goodness* is one of God's attributes and a grace He promises to His people. Read Exodus 33:12-23, an amazing scene between God and His servant Moses.

   ⤝ What was Moses' request in verse 18?

⚥ Why (verses 12-17)?

⚥ What was God's response to His timid servant (verse 19)?

⚥ And in Exodus 34:6?

⚥ What do you learn about God's goodness from this verse?

⚥ And from Psalm 31:19?

⚥ And from Psalm 100:5?

2. **God's Continued Mercy.** *Mercy* is another of God's attributes and another of His graces that He promises we, as His people, will enjoy. In the following scriptures what do you learn about God's mercy and the hope His mercy brings?

⚥ Exodus 33:18-19 and 34:6—

⚥ Psalm 100:5—

✖ Psalm 103:4—

✖ Lamentations 3:22-23—

✖ Titus 3:5—

3. **God's Continued Pursuit.** David explains that God's goodness and mercy will "follow" him. These two solid, dependable qualities of the Lord will most assuredly "follow after" and "pursue" and "accompany" David. How vigorously? As vigorously as David's enemies pursued him!

   ✖ How did this promise bring hope to David's life?

   ✖ How does it bring hope to you?

4. **God's Continued Presence.**

   ✖ How long does David say God's goodness and mercy will pursue him?

   ✖ How does this promise bring hope to David's life?

   ✖ And to yours?

Your Moment with the Shepherd

1. Throughout our walk with the Shepherd in Psalm 23 we've focused on what we consider to be needs and God's gracious provision for those needs.

   ∾ What present difficulties are you dealing with?

   ∾ How does God's goodness and mercy provide hope and encouragement in your trials?

2. What possible future problems are you likely to encounter?

   ∾ How does the thought of God's goodness and mercy encourage you as you think about these problems?

3. Jesus commanded, "Do not worry about your life" (Matthew 6:25). Take a minute to evaluate yourself in this area of anxiety over the daily demands and circumstances of life. Rate yourself on a 1 to 10 worry scale (10 being really worried) and note how your behavior relates to Jesus' command to not worry.

   ∾ How will David's statement of hope ("Surely goodness and mercy shall follow me all the days of my life") help you comply with Jesus' charge in Matthew 6:25?

   ∾ And Matthew 6:34?

Hope is not to be seen as an uncertainty. We are not hoping that God's promises will come true. No, we have confident hope in God's promises because we have confidence in the character of God. A promise is only as good as the one who makes it. Because of God's goodness and mercy, we can be confident that He will follow through on what He promises!

12

God's Home Is Yours...
Forever!

Just mention the word *home* and our minds tend to race toward decorating, organizing, and cleaning. We think about the nest we're creating for our loved ones. Magazines like *House Beautiful* and *Better Homes and Gardens* quickly come to mind. What does the Bible say about "home"?

Seven Reasons for Hope in the Future

1. What are the four "Reasons for Hope in the Future" we've already discussed?

5. **Eternal Worship.** The desire to worship God resides at the core of every believer's heart and soul. We adore our God and yearn to express that adoration. Our souls long to praise Him, and our lips long to join in with joyful thanksgiving.

David wrote, "I will dwell in the house of the Lord forever." Throughout his life David longed *for* God and longed to *be with* God. His words expressed a deep desire for the continual presence of God and the realization of constant communion with Him. What can we learn about the "house of the LORD" and about David's desires from these verses?

   ✎ Psalm 26:8—

✒ Psalm 27:4—

✒ What did other biblical writers note about "the house of the Lord"?

- Psalm 84:4—

- Psalm 100:3 and 4—

6. Eternal Home. David spent much of his life on the move.

1. How and where did David live a great deal of his life?

   ✒ 1 Samuel 22:1—

   ✒ 1 Samuel 24:1-3—

   ✒ 1 Samuel 26:1-3—

   ✒ 2 Samuel 15:27-28—

2. How does the psalmist refer to himself in Psalm 119:19?

3. And how does Peter refer to all Christians (1 Peter 2:11)?

4. What does Jesus tell us about "home" (John 14:2-3)?

7. **Eternal Presence.** The greatest blessing in every believer's life
   will be that of eternal, intimate fellowship with God—being in
   His presence forever. We live for it, we long for it, and we look
   forward to it.

   ⤳ How does Psalm 84:1-2 express the longings of the
   soul for God's eternal presence?

   ⤳ And how does Revelation 21:3-4 explain God's eternal
   presence and our experience in His presence?

   ⤳ What (or Who!) awaits us in heaven, according to
   Hebrews 8:1?

Eternal worship, an eternal home, and eternal presence! We are most
blessed by these divine promises! David desired the fullness of joy
and the forevermore pleasures of the Lord's presence in a forevermore home. And the same is true of you and me.

Your Moment with the Shepherd
It's obvious as David closes Psalm 23 with "the house of the LORD" in
mind that he was consumed with God and the thought of enjoying
an eternal home with Him.

1. How do you think these practices will help you be "consumed" with the Lord? How would they better prepare you to be with God forever?

   ⤳ Matthew 6:19-21—

   ⤳ Colossians 3:1—

   ⤳ Colossians 3:2—

   ⤳ Hebrews 10:25—

2. Meet Anna. She desired eternal worship, an eternal home, and the eternal presence of God. She also teaches us how to be consumed with God. Read her story in Luke 2:36-38, keeping in mind that she was probably a woman who had no kin.

   ⤳ How did Anna choose to live out the days of her earthly existence? And which of the three reasons for hope did this choice fulfill?

   ⤳ Where did Anna choose to live out her days? And which two of the three reasons for hope did this choice fulfill?

   ⤳ What did Anna do that instructs us on what it means to

be consumed in the here-and-now with God while we wait for the hereafter?

⤳ What can you do to live more like Anna and be more consumed with God and His promises?

3. Look again at Revelation 21:3-4. What about this scene causes you to yearn for a home in heaven?

4. How deeply do you long for heaven?

⤳ What can you do to move your desire closer to David's desire to dwell in the house of the Lord forever?

5. Of the 12 promises described in Psalm 23, which one or ones give you the greatest assurance as you face the future?

These 12 promises from Psalm 23 are promises for a lifetime. But, dear one, there are more—many more!—promises available to you as you trek through life. The more you study God's Word, the more hope and joy you'll have. Keep in the Word!

Notes

God Is Your Confidence, Hope, and Joy
1. Ray and Anne Ortlund, *The Best Half of Life* (Glendale, CA: Regal Books, 1976), 88.
2. Carole Mayhall, *From the Heart of a Woman* (Colorado Springs: NavPress, 1976), 10-11.

Chapter 1—God Cares for You
1. Arnold A. Dallimore, *Susanna Wesley, the Mother of John and Charles Wesley* (Grand Rapids, MI: Baker Book House, 1994), 15.

Chapter 2—God Will Always Provide
1. www.cbaonline.org/voice/back_list_main.htm, 5/24/99.
2. A. Naismith, *A Treasury of Notes, Quotes, and Anecdotes* (Grand Rapids, MI: Baker Book House, 1976), 216.
3. *Life Application Bible—The Living Bible* (Wheaton, IL: Tyndale House Publishers, Inc., 1988), 42.
4. Curtis Vaughan, gen. ed., *The Old Testament Books of Poetry from 26 Translations* (Grand Rapids, MI: Zondervan Bible Publishers, 1973), 189. Versions cited, in order: PBV, HAR, JERUS, BAS, TAY.
5. G. Campbell Morgan, *Life Applications from Every Chapter of the Bible* (Grand Rapids, MI: Fleming H. Revell, 1994), 159.

Chapter 3—God Gives You Rest
1. J.I. Packer, quoted in Albert M. Wells, Sr., ed., *Inspiring Quotations—Contemporary & Classical* (Nashville: Thomas Nelson Publishers, 1988), 15.
2. "Seven Minutes with God" from the ministry of the Navigators, Colorado Springs, CO.
3. Wells, *Inspiring Quotations,* 17.
4. W.G. Bowen, *Why! The Shepherd!* (c/o Mavis Bowen, Dansey Road, RD2, Rotorua, Nth Island, N.Z.), 30-31.
5. Vaughan, *The Old Testament Books of Poetry,* 189.

Chapter 4—God's Peace Is Always Available to You
1. Frances R. Havergal, "Like a River Glorious," 1876.
2. E.W. Blandy, "Where He Leads Me," 1890.

Chapter 5—God Is Your Healer

1. W.G. Bowen, *Why! The Shepherd!* (c/o Mavis Bowen, Dansey Road, RD2, Rotorua, Nth Island, N.Z.), 50-51.
2. Ibid., 52.
3. Ibid., 55.
4. H. Edwin Young, *The Lord Is...* (Nashville: Broadman Press, 1981), 36.

Chapter 6—God Will Guide You

1. Elizabeth George, *Beautiful in God's Eyes—The Treasures of the Proverbs 31 Woman* (Eugene, OR: Harvest House Publishers, 1998), 205.
2. Robert Alden, *Psalms—Songs of Devotion,* vol. 1 (Chicago: Moody Press, 1974), 60.

Chapter 7—God Never Leaves You

1. Carole C. Carlson, *Corrie ten Boom: Her Life, Her Faith* (Old Tappan, NJ: Fleming H. Revell, 1983), 219.
2. Mrs. Charles E. Cowman, *Streams in the Desert,* vol. 2 (Grand Rapids, MI: Zondervan Publishing House, 1966), 34.
3. Source unknown.
4. John Charles Pollock, *Hudson Taylor and Maria* (New York: McGraw-Hill, 1962), 206.
5. Mrs. Howard Taylor, *John and Betty Stam—A Story of Triumph* (Chicago: Moody Press, 1982), 80.
6. Adapted from the song "Finally Home," author unknown.
7. Cowman, *Streams in the Desert,* vol. 1 (Grand Rapids, MI: Zondervan Publishing House, 1965), 52.

Chapter 8—God's Comfort Is Only a Prayer Away

1. Herbert Lockyer, *All the Divine Names and Titles in the Bible* (Grand Rapids, MI: Zondervan Publishing House, 1980), 10.
2. F.B. Meyer, source unknown.
3. J. Allen Blair, *Living Reliantly—A Devotional Study of the 23rd Psalm* (Neptune, NJ: Loizeaux Brothers, 1980), 83.

Chapter 9—God Is Your Friend...and So Much More

1. Naismith, *1200 Notes, Quotes, and Anecdotes,* 48.
2. M.R. DeHaan and Henry G. Bosch, *Our Daily Bread,* quoting H.W. Baker (Grand Rapids, MI: Zondervan Publishing House, 1982), January 26.

Chapter 10—God Will Always Protect You

1. Frances R. Havergal, "Like a River Glorious," 1876.

Chapter 11—God Is Your Hope

1. Herbert Lockyer, *All the Promises of the Bible* (Grand Rapids, MI: Zondervan Publishing House, 1962), 10.
2. Curtis Vaughan, gen. ed., *The New Testament from 26 Translations,* The New English Bible (Grand Rapids, MI: Zondervan Publishing, 1967), 1161.
3. Susan H. Peterson, "Do Not Worry," 1998. Released into public domain, found at www.cyberhymnal.org.
4. Alexander Maclaren, *Exposition of Holy Scripture, Psalms* (Grand Rapids, MI: Baker Book House, 1982), 103.

Chapter 12—God's Home Is Yours...Forever!

1. Paul Lee Tan, *Encyclopedia of 7,700 Illustrations* (Winona Lake, IN: BMH Books, 1979), 1442-43.
2. E.M. Blaiklock, *Commentary on the Psalms,* vol. 1 (Philadelphia: A.J. Holman Company, 1977), 63.
3. D.L. Moody, *Notes from My Bible and Thoughts from My Library* (Grand Rapids, MI: Baker Book House, 1979), 66.

Questions and Insights for Deeper Understanding and Discussion

1. Roy B. Zuck, *Speaker's Quote Book* (Grand Rapids, MI: Kregel Publications, 1997), p. 170.
2. John MacArthur, *MacArthur Study Bible* (Nashville: Word Publishing, 1997), 1916.
3. Matthew Henry, *Commentary on the Whole Bible,* vol. 3 (Peabody, MA: Hendrickson Publishers, 1996), 258.
4. MacArthur, *MacArthur Study Bible,* 1224.

BIBLE STUDIES *for* BUSY WOMEN

Character Studies

Old Testament Studies

New Testament Studies

A WOMAN AFTER GOD'S OWN HEART® BIBLE STUDIES

*E*lizabeth takes women step-by-step through the Scriptures, sharing wisdom she's gleaned from more than 30 years as a women's Bible teacher.

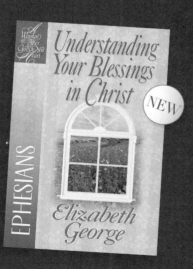

NEW

• MINUTE FOR BUSY WOMEN •

Elizabeth George can also be heard on the radio with her feature "A Woman After God's Own Heart."

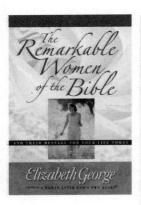

The Remarkable Women of the Bible

Come and see how God enabled ordinary women to live extraordinary lives. How? By turning their weaknesses into strengths, their sorrows into joys, and their despair into hope. Along the way you'll learn great truths about God...

- From Eve you'll see God is faithful even when you fail
- From Sarah you'll find God always keeps His promises
- From Rebekah you'll discover God has a plan for your life

What made these women—and many others—so remarkable? They loved god passionately, looked to Him in life's daily challenges, and yielded to His transforming grace. And you can enjoy God's miraculous work in your life today...by following in their footsteps!

For additional, more in-depth study, *The Remarkable Women of the Bible Growth and Study Guide* is also available.

Books by Elizabeth George

- Beautiful in God's Eyes
- Finding God's Path Through Your Trials
- Following God with All Your Heart
- Life Management for Busy Women
- Loving God with All Your Mind
- A Mom After God's Own Heart
- Powerful Promises for Every Woman
- The Remarkable Women of the Bible
- Small Changes for a Better Life
- Walking with the Women of the Bible
- A Wife After God's Own Heart
- A Woman After God's Own Heart®
- A Woman After God's Own Heart® Deluxe Edition
- A Woman After God's Own Heart®—A Daily Devotional
- A Woman After God's Own Heart® Collection
- A Woman's Call to Prayer
- A Woman's High Calling
- A Woman's Walk with God
- A Young Woman After God's Own Heart
- A Young Woman After God's Own Heart—A Devotional
- A Young Woman's Call to Prayer
- A Young Woman's Walk with God

Study Guides

- Beautiful in God's Eyes Growth & Study Guide
- Finding God's Path Through Your Trials Growth & Study Guide
- Following God with All Your Heart Growth & Study Guide
- Life Management for Busy Women Growth & Study Guide
- Loving God with All Your Mind Growth & Study Guide
- A Mom After God's Own Heart Growth & Study Guide
- The Remarkable Women of the Bible Growth & Study Guide
- Small Changes for a Better Life Growth & Study Guide
- Understanding Your Blessings in Christ
- A Wife After God's Own Heart Growth & Study Guide
- A Woman After God's Own Heart® Growth & Study Guide
- A Woman's Call to Prayer Growth & Study Guide
- A Woman's High Calling Growth & Study Guide
- A Woman's Walk with God Growth & Study Guide

Children's Books

- God's Wisdom for Little Girls
- A Little Girl After God's Own Heart

Books by Jim & Elizabeth George

- God Loves His Precious Children
- God's Wisdom for Little Boys
- A Little Boy After God's Own Heart

Books by Jim George

- The Bare Bones Bible® Handbook
- The Bare Bones Bible® Handbook for Teens
- The Bare Bones Bible® Bios
- A Husband After God's Own Heart
- A Man After God's Own Heart
- The Remarkable Prayers of the Bible
- A Young Man After God's Own Heart

Elizabeth George...

is a bestselling author and speaker whose passion is to teach the Bible in a way that changes women's lives. She has more than 4.9 million books in print, including *A Woman After God's Own Heart* and *Remarkable Women of the Bible*.

For information about Elizabeth's books or speaking ministry, to sign up for her mailings, or to purchase Elizabeth's books, please contact her at:

www.ElizabethGeorge.com

or

1-800-542-4611

or

Elizabeth George
P.O. Box 2879
Belfair, WA 98528